The Fast Lane

Hard to Get Caught, Easy to get **Caught Up**

BY

TASHBINA WAHID

Table of Contents

Dedication

I would like to dedicate the *Fast Lane*
to my Lord and Savior.

Thank You for sparing my life and loving me
more than I love myself.

I'm thankful to be the angel you left behind.

*It is during our darkest moments that
we must focus to see the light.*
—Aristotle Onassis

To: Amandeep ☺

The choices you chose today,
you have to live with
tomorrow.....

love

Buckle Up

The woman that everyone knows, but not everyone knows about. An easy smile and welcoming eyes, **but what's behind those windows? She didn't ta**ke the perfect path, but every event was a brick in the road that has brought her to where she is today. That past is now an open book, all the despair, all the tragedy, and all the heartbreak. Who is Tashbina Wahid? Now is your opportunity to find out. Come and experience life in the Fast Lane!

Decatur Girl

I was born in Albany, New York. I don't have a lot of memories of the place, but I've been back a few times, and never for happy occasions. I remember broken streets and crowded corners, and it seemed like every other person had a disease or looked sick. To this day, I don't know what the specifics of the situation were, but I assume we left for Georgia so my mom could get away from my dad. He was strung out on drugs, abusive, and a regular at the local jail. From the little I know, I'm glad my mom moved me and my sister down to Atlanta to start her life over. I'm still thanking her to this day.

When we got to Atlanta, we moved to Decatur to live with my Granddaddy and G-mama, but that didn't last long. My mom didn't have the best relationship with my Grandaddy's wife at the time, so she packed up and moved us to some apartments across from the drive-in liquor store on Glenwood. They were so ghetto and project, but she did the best she could with what she had. She always made us feel like everything was fine. She did our hair every other night, and kept us looking cute. We also stayed at the thrift store. Our favorite was the thrift store in Belvedere plaza on Memorial Drive. We'd hit them up every Monday because that's the day they had the special red and green tag sales. We would leave out of there with five and six bags like we was really balling and my mom had only spent $50 (lol).

It seemed like ever since we moved from Grandaddy's house, my mom had more motivation not to fail. My Grand dad always tried to help us as much as he could, and thankfully my mom and G momma relationship got better. My mom enrolled in hair school at Dekalb Tech while working at the hospital. I don't know how she did it, so many long nights studying then having to get up and go right to work. I can appreciate all her sweat and tears now that I'm grown. Anything worth having isn't easy.

We moved to at least three different apartments on Glenwood, and I didn't know it then, but every time we moved it was to a better apartment each time. A little less run-down, roach-infested, crackhead-living each time. I remember the day my mom came home and was so excited: we had got approved for Section 8 and she had found us a cute little house on Ledo Avenue big enough to fit us. We had a yard for the first time ever, even a mailbox. We finally had a real place to call home, even our own mailbox.

The house at 1775 Ledo was very small, white with pink framing. It had a front yard to match, and a big back yard.

I remember it having a beat up brown fence, a small car port just big enough for the car we didn't have. The street was pretty peaceful, and we had a handful of neighbors that we talked to. To the right of us was Mr. and Mrs. Porter, an old white couple that were very independent. They cut their own grass, and even though we always used to run through their yard to get to the next, they were never mean to us and gave us candy all the time. The next two families that lived by them were Laotian, and were cousins and neighbors, Tina and Laok Dog. We would play together, then beat each other up, then not talk for days. They were my best friends. I had previously went to Snapfinger Elementary, but it was only briefly, because after we'd been approved for Section 8, I started attending Atherton Elementary on Glenwood.

Even though it wasn't the best school, Atherton also wasn't the worst, either. The teachers there were really genuine. It seemed like they loved to teach. I had gained another best friend, Meka, whom I had met in Ms. Robert's third grade class, and we're still friends to this day. We made some of the same crazy decisions later in life. Meanwhile things were looking up for my mom. The people at Dekalb Medical Center really loved that she was a hard worker and respected that she was taking care of two girls. Sometimes they let us come to the hospital and volunteer. My sister and I were both candy stripers. We wore long red and white dresses with white polo shirts underneath and the little shoes they used to call white girls. I guess us helping out at the hospital made me have a love for volunteering, and giving back to the community. I looked forward to going to work with my mom every summer, bringing flowers to sick patients, and even bringing crackers and water to the rude ones. I knew they were only mean because their family members never came to see them.

Despite working full time, going to school part time, and taking care of me and my sister, my mom never seemed to get down about her situation. I remember one particular morning when she seemed extra happy, though. She was singing while she was cleaning. Around that time my sister and I started noticing a small, red pickup truck in the evenings after she had put us to bed.

Weeks passed, and while we didn't have all the facts, we knew that our mom's smile was golden. One evening, my mom had made us one of her famous Southern meals, friend chicken, and collard greens with smoked turkey, macaroni and cheese, with some jiffy corn bread, that sweet corn bread that tasted like pound cake. We were sitting at dinner, and she mentioned to us that she had met an amazing man and his name was Mr. Lee.

I asked, "Are you talking about the man in the red truck that always picks you up?"

"Yes, nosey," she stated. She told us that Mr. Lee had no kids, had never been married, and lived on McAfee road, not too far from the Candler Road Flea Market. He had a big family and was a custodian at fine restaurants in Atlanta, like Houston's and Copeland's .My sister and I didn't know what all that meant at the time, but we did know that whoever this Mr. Lee was, he needed to stick around.

On our first meeting with Mr. Lee, I remember him favoring Mr. Rogers. Mr. Lee was dark skinned, very, very slim, and always wore button down shirts and high wasted pants. He tied his shoe laces so tight, I thought his feet were going to suffocate. He seemed as nervous as we were to meet him. I guess because people always want to feel accepted and not like they have to prove themselves. The meeting went fine though, and after that our lives started changing quickly. We had more groceries in the fridge, he helped my mom get her first car, and cut our grass every week.

It was a Saturday morning on our front porch when I finally got up the guts to ask my mom how she met Mr. Lee. Mom said that she had went out with one of her good friends Debra and they had stopped at the Shell on Covington Highway and Memorial to get cigarettes. Mr. Lee had pulled up to the pump to get gas and she immediately noticed his fly car. It was a 1985 brown and black corvette, and even though Lee wasn't super cool, the car made him look cooler. She told me that she went over to him once her friend had gone into the store, and she complimented him on his car. They talked briefly and he asked her if she wanted to get something to eat. My mom's favorite restaurant "This Is It" on Memorial Drive was right across the street, so she ditched Debra and got in the car with Lee. This part is so funny because my mom said Lee had a no-smoking sign in his corvette. She lit up a cigarette, then asked if it was okay if she smoked. He liked her so much, he didn't care. Before they left the restaurant, she got some chitlins to go. Right as he was headed to take her home, they drove over a speed bump and all the chitlins, along with the juice, spilled in that man's car. The date was over after that. I was sitting in tears laughing at my mom. If I was Mr. Lee, I would've wanted to just push her out of the car, along with her chitlins. But she told me he called her the next day, so I guess after all that he still saw the potential. My mom had also stated that he didn't want kids, didn't like a woman that smoke or drank, or used profanity. My mom was all the above, had two kids and smoked, sometimes other things on special occasions. She even drank wine and margaritas when she had long days at work. Maybe the statement is true that opposites attract.

Mr. Lee took us under his wing and loved us like we were his own. He taught my sister how to drive, and also helped her get her first car. Also, slowly but surely, my mom was helping him become more stylish. Behind his back, I was still calling Mr. Lee Mr. Rogers, and my mom would pop me in the mouth every time I called him that.

Even though my sister and Mr. Lee had developed a pretty good relationship, her and my mother's relationship was starting to go downhill. I'm not sure if it was the people she was hanging out with in high school that was causing it or if it was some kind of bad connection between my mom and my sister at that age. My mom and her mother relationship wasn't the best, and my mom had stopped living with her mother as a teenager. I guess they also say like mother like daughter.

I remember when my sister got her first job at Ingles. She was ecstatic and ready for work, but it wasn't the best fit, plus her coworkers were jealous of her. She had immediately started applying at other places and got a job at K-Mart. She had also met this guy named Rodney who was a little older than her, and really started disobeying my mother. Rodney was obviously a cheater, so that didn't last long, and she moved on to a popular basketball player named Tim. Everyone thought they were the perfect couple. He seemed very nice, but I hated his nose, which had a smushed down look that made it seem like he couldn't breathe. He did have waves that made us seasick, and other than his nose he was kind of cute.

One stormy night, I was asleep in bed and my sister was on the phone talking to her boyfriend Taz. My mom picked up the phone and whatever she heard was enough to run into the room and snatch the phone from my sister and start a horrible fight. In the end, my sister ended up grabbing her things and storming out. She said she was never coming back, and she never did. For awhile I didn't see her, and after I got to high school, the only time I saw her was in school, but regardless of everything that was going on, she still graduated top of her class and was honored Miss Towers High. I always have admired my sister for so many reasons, graduated from one of the best schools in Georgia which was UGA, got married then had kids, and now a store owner and one of the ambassadors for OWN.

Not long after that my mom received a notice that we no longer qualified for Section 8 assistance and my mom and Mr. Lee started looking for a new house. After a couple of weeks they found a cute brick house on a corner lot with pink shutters and a double car port. When we finally moved in, it felt like we were a family.

The neighborhood was an upgrade from the one on Ledo. It was an actual subdivision, Pendley Hills Estates off of Covington Highway, one street over from Glenwood. It was funny, we did all that moving, and never ended up very far from where he started. Some of my good friends were Key, Leslie, Chris, Frankie, and Tasha. I had a big crush on this guy named J Hunter. His family stayed two blocks up and I used to walk by their house twice or maybe three times a day, hoping to see him walk to his car or checking the mailbox. They lived not too far from the candy lady so of course I begged my mom all the time for a $1.50 so I could get the Koolaid icies that came in the small, white cups, hot fries and bubble gum.

I transferred to a school named Rowland after we moved, but I was only there a year until it was time to make the transition to high school. All my friends from Rowland were nervous about going to high school. I remember being excited. I had cut my own hair myself and when I realized I messed it up, I put it back into a ponytail two days before school started. My mom cursed me out and put me on punishment as usual for not doing things when told. She threatened not to let me wear my new clothes to school, and was going to make me wear my old clothes from the previous year. There was no way I could to high school looking like elementary. I was finally there with my sister and the big dogs. Plus I couldn't wait to see my old bffs from Ledo Avenue, which were Laok and Tina.

My outfit the first day was a white, sleeveless top with a lime green short skirt and my favorite white platform soda shoes. To this day my friends still laugh at me about those shoes. Everybody hated them, and I loved them. I had cut my own hair and my mom didn't take me to the hair salon to fix it, so I had short on the top, long on the back, and gapped in the middle. That was another punishment of mine for doing what I wanted to do.

I became popular fast in high school. I was one of those people who could adapt to anyone around me and any environment, so I had friends that was bougie, super ghetto, and in between. Plus my sister was a senior and everyone that knew her, knew me. She had paved a path for me to be successful in high school. She was captain of the drill team, on the swim team, and in various clubs. She was very stylish, had a shape that many admired, plus was very book smart. She later got accepted into UGA and did it all while not living at home. Even though her and mom's relationship struggled, a lot of people supported my sister because of her hard work and persistence to never fail.

So I started making my own way in high school. I got good grades, was on the soccer team. I tried out for the drill team but never got on (lol), so I just danced in the stands at the football games. By sophomore year I was dating this guy who was two years older than me. His name was Nard, and everyone called him Sirloin. He was brown skinned, husky, and such a gentleman. By then I also wanted to get a job because my mom wasn't giving me enough money.

I applied everywhere, Kroger, Publix, summer camps, and all the shoe stores. I was very persistent because I wanted my own money. I guess I was considered a bugaboo to them, but I didn't care. I was going to show up until someone said yes. My hard work eventually paid off, too. The fourth time I went to the footlocker in Avondale Mall, the manager Derek asked me why I wanted to work there so bad. I told him because I was getting old enough to work, wanted my own money, and that I was pretty responsible. He wasn't supposed to hire me until I was actually 16, but he slipped me through the system. That next year that store closed down and they transferred me to the location in South Dekalb Mall.

Me and Nard's relationship continued to grow, as well, and things were going pretty well until I missed my cycle. Nard's family had loved me and been very supportive, but knowing that I was pregnant, I wasn't sure how they would react. My mom had a tendency of loving us and cursing us out at the same damn time. Me and Nard decided to tell my mom and the conversation didn't go so well. She cursed us both, kicked him out, and told me that we were having her grandbaby.

Nard and I knew we weren't ready, though. We had to decide if we were really going to keep it, or abort and live with that horrible decision. The days became long and dreadful, because I knew that I had to make a decision and had to make it quick. I'd heard so many cruel comments about women who had abortions, but I'd also seen so many teenage mothers struggle while trying to make it through high school. I decided that plan b was my best option. Nard was a true gentleman, soft spoken, loved me, and supported me in whatever decision I made. Meanwhile I continued to go to work and school.

By Monday of the big week, I had googled abortion clinics and had made the decision that I'd have the procedure that Friday. I had told a few people about my situation, like my friend Key and one of my close teachers, Colonel King from my ROTC class. He was very disappointed because he thought so highly of me.

That Wednesday was a long day at school, and I still had to go to Foot Locker. Once I got there, I noticed that I started feeling funny, very light headed and just not my normal self. My manager told me to go chill out. Right before closing, I noticed that I had to keep using the restroom, and the very last time I went, I noticed spotting. I immediately started freaking out, because I knew I wasn't supposed to bleed while pregnant. I didn't want my manager to know what was going on, so I did my best not to make any phone calls until I got to my car. When I finally got outside and started dialing, though, I immediately hung up. I didn't know what to do, but my conscience was telling me that something was very, very wrong.

When I walked through the front door, I saw my mom was in the den watching TV.

"Hey mom, had a long day, going to bed," I said. I started to go downstairs when I felt what I thought was a blood clot pass through me. I rushed into the bathroom.

As soon as I pulled down my underwear, the baby fell right into the toilet. I started crying. I screamed out my mom's name and she ran into the bathroom. She started crying then, too.

We fished my baby out of the toilet with a plastic bag, then rushed to Dekalb Medical, where they admitted me to the ER and plugged me up to so many machines. Hours later they came back and told me I had a life-threatening miscarriage. I was feeling very crazy because of how everything went down. Even though I had planned to have an abortion, how I ended up losing the baby still made me depressed. I didn't attend school for two days because the doctor recommended that I stay home and let my body rest. Colonel King called to check on me and made sure everything was okay. Key called me after she got out of school, and I had to tell her why I had missed school.

As soon as I got better, my mom wrote down a list of things to do to make sure I didn't get pregnant again. From that point, everything went haywire. Most people my age had time for hanging out with friends, but my life had become school, work, chores, and sleep. I didn't even have time to see Nard, but he was determined to make our relationship work. The time we spent together at school became crucial, and sometimes he would come to Foot Locker on my breaks. He always made me a priority. My mom on the other hand was starting to drive me crazy. Even though

I had put myself in a bad situation, I didn't deserve to be treated like a criminal. After hearing "If you don't like it, get the hell out," everyday, all day, one Saturday morning I decided to get the hell out.

I called Nard's mom, crying, and let her know that it was time for me to go, and asked if I could live with them until things had gotten better. She told me she'd had Nard pick me up. I hung up and proceeded upstairs to tell my mom that I thought it was best for me to leave. I felt that I was going to be trapped in the house for the rest of my high school years. I could see myself missing all the Friday night football games, not being able to see my favorite basketball players play, not being able to play soccer when I was already reigning MVP, and wouldn't have had any chance of being Miss Towers High. I was standing right in front of my mom having that conversation, thinking of all the stuff that could happen and why there so many reasons to get the hell on. I realize now that this is the point of my life when I became someone who ran from her problems.

My mom looked at me probably how she had looked at my sister. "Oh, so you really think you grown enough to be out on your own? You growing hair on your pussy, you getting some titties, and you think you grown. Well if you think you grown enough to be on your own, get the hell out. Oh, and by the way, where you going?"

I told her that I was going to live with Nard and his mom. She said some things to me then that I prefer not to repeat, pushed me out of the way and went to the kitchen. She took a box of trash bags into my room and started putting all my clothes, shoes, accessories, everything I owned into those garbage bags. By the time Nard pulled up, I had twenty something trash bags on the lawn, and I was sitting on them and crying.

"What the hell," he said after he got out.

"Exactly, please hurry and get me out of here," I said.

He put all the bags in the back of his truck and we pulled off. I was a sophomore in high school and that's when I left home for the last time.

When we pulled up to his mom's apartment at Hidden Creek on Young Road, I was nervous, sad, depressed, all the above. His mom greeted me with a big hug and told me to wipe my tears, and regardless of what happened, her and Nard were there for me and I had nothing to worry about. She was very kind and treated me like I was the daughter she never had. To this day my mother would say that was the worst mistake a mother could make, letting a young girl and boy live together under the same roof. I guess his mom didn't have time to think things through. She just made a hasty decision that it was okay for me to stay. I'm not sure if she thought of us having sex in his bedroom or even me getting pregnant again. I never found out if she knew about the first pregnancy.

Living there was quite a bit different from my mother's. Even though I had the peace of mind of my mom not yelling or cursing or giving me chores, it also wasn't peaches and cream. When Nard was away, his mom and boyfriend argued a lot, and sometimes I was scared he would hit her. I would shut the door, turn the music up loud, and even blast the TV to avoid hearing the disrespectful manner. I could understand what a young child felt like when their parents argued. I didn't know what was going on, I just knew that I was scared. My mom and Lee never argued, and all of their disagreements they worked out.

I didn't know if I should talk to Nard about his mom's business. I wanted to avoid tension. She was giving me a place to stay and I was finally getting the chance to spend time with Nard. Eventually, his mom left that guy and that apartment, and we moved into a cute little house in a neighborhood near club Mirage. She also went back to her old school fling Alton. You know how those old school women are. They'd rather go back to the cheating ass dog and old bullshit and try to make it work rather than date someone new. She might have a prosperous future with a new guy, but she's unsure of the shit and baggage that new guy has. She'll take ten steps backwards and stick with the devil she knows.

Things went smoothly for a quick two months and then the arguing came back. It seemed like she had a pattern of dating men who didn't make her happy. I missed my mom and Lee desperately. I missed my family period. I had run from my problems at home and found elsewhere.

Nard had gone off to the military and started to not come home every weekend. So I was living in that house with all the arguing, and I still wasn't getting to see Nard. I made the decision that it was time to leave. I said thanks to his mom for all the love and support and as I walked out the door I turned back. She was at the dinner table just looking down. I thought to myself that I hoped she became a stronger woman and realized her self-worth. She deserved to be happy.

Meeting Daro

This chapter of my life was the most life changing, heartfelt, and tragic time ever.

Even though it has been several years now, everything still feels like yesterday and still now I shed tears writing. It all started the summer I graduated from Towers. I was feeling great about life, had graduated with a 3.7, was the queen, Ms Towers High, MVP two years running for soccer. I was a little sad that Nard was still in Kuwait (Nard was the older guy I dated while in high school but he graduated three years before I did and went off to the military). He was my first love (puppy love). When I realized he was gonna be gone longer than we thought, my feelings started shifting away. It was Friday night and time to hit up Golden Glide. If you're from Decatur, you know all about skating, Glenwood day, the old Freak Nics.

Me and Key went to the rink that night. I had picked her up in old faithful my hatchback white Ford Escort (lol y'all remember that car oh yeah it was in the homecoming parade don't hate!!!). As we pulled up to Golden Glide, we realized how long the line was and almost turned around, but didn't cause we had bought new fits at South Dekalb Mall earlier that day, so we had to show the new fits! We stepped in the building saying hey to all the regulars, smiling at the new cuties and dissing the had beens! Got in the crazy long line to get the whack skates they give you, hoping one day to get the fly skates all the good skaters had.

Finally on the floor, the DJ was jamming that night. I was dancing in my skates like nobody's business when a tall guy with dreads and golds bumped me. I act like I didn't feel it (I love playing hard to get, I guess that's what made me different from the other thirsty girls). I knew my self-worth and demanded more, so I kept on skating like I didn't feel anything.

And at first, I really didn't notice him. He was tall, with dreads, mouth full of gold teeth. I looked, but kept it moving. A little later he caught up with me on the floor, and he was confident.

He said, "Oh, so you gone act like that?" and after that we talked for a bit, and exchanged numbers. You know how it is, sometimes you're out and you meet people, have conversation. They get your number, or give you theirs. I wasn't expecting anything to come of it right then. He said he was going to call me for breakfast, and at the time I was thinkin "Yeah right."

I left before he did, and when I saw him from my car in the parking lot, I watched him to see what he was drivin. Daro stepped up to this sky-blue, beat-up, granddaddy van, and I thought "OMG." I thought that, but there was still something about the way he carried himself. He was hood, but still stylish. He drove that van, but…

So I had to smile when Daro called me the next morning about breakfast, like he said he would.

"Okay, where you wanna meet?" I asked him.

"Waffle King," he said. "You know the one on Flat Shoals." Now, I hadn't ever eaten at a Waffle King, and didn't know what to think at his suggestion. Still, I said yes.

I was early for our first date, sitting inside and waiting to see if he was going to pull up in that granddaddy van. And he did. I remember thinkin to myself, "This must really be his car."

When he came inside, I could see that he had tags hanging offa his clothes.

"You know you got tags hangin from your clothes," I said. He looked down at himself.

"Oh, my bad," he said, and then just casually ripped them off his clothes and handed them to a waitress that was walking by. I couldn't believe how ghetto he was. However, even though he had the golds, and the van, all of it, we hit it off. He was something different from the guy I would've normally dated back then. Breakfast was nice.

At the end of it, he asked, "What else you got goin on today?"

I was still working at the Foot Locker in South Dekalb Mall, and I needed to pick up my check. When I told him that, he offered to drive me, and I accepted.

When I looked into his van, it was a little spooky. The inside was dark: dark carpet, dark paneling, low lighting. As he drove away, I asked him about his van.

"I got another car I'm fixin up," he said. "An old school cutlass." So I was like okay, that made sense.

So we get to the mall, and as soon as we walk in, I'm noticing that people are dapping him up and calling his name. Daro, they said, or Twin. Daro had a brother who looked just like him, which is why they sometimes called him twin. His street name was Turk. Even though they looked alike, they had two different personalities. Daro was more passive, the nice one that always smiled, and would give you the shirt off his back. Turk was more of the all-business, more likely to take the shirt off of your back if you had handled him the wrong way. Turk dated a young lady by the name Nita. Nita was light skinned, always wore long hair, and had a really cute shape. Some people knew her for the flowers below her waist and was one of the best dancer's at Jazzy T's. When he was locked up for a few months, she was there, and there all the mess that he put her through, she still stayed loyal. That true ride of die chick.

"He must be a street guy," I thought to myself. How else could everybody know him? Even still, we spent the rest of the day together, and the most of a lot of days after that. Looking back, I realize I was so green to the game that I didn't even see that he was makin plays while we were hangin out all those days. He would drive me around, and stop by this house, go in and out real quick, or stop by that gas station. I never knew who he was meeting, and in the beginning I didn't know why.

Months passed like that, before this one particular day.

I don't know what they're called now, but back then they were the Green Isle Apartments. Daro picked me up around 8, and I told him I wanted to get to the nail shop before it closed at 9.

"Man," he said, "I gotta make this play right fast."

I had an attitude with him, because I really wanted to get to the place before it closed. I even asked him again.

"After my play."

So we pull into Green Isle and stop by the mail boxes in the front. I could see a man waiting there for Daro. Real quick, he jumped out of the van, walked over to the guy, and exchanged some things.

Right then police jumped out from everywhere. They were yelling at Daro for him to stop where he was standing and lay on the ground. From the van, I could see they had a beam on him.

"What the fuck, oh my god," I said. I was so scared and nervous.

But Daro didn't stop. He ran back to the van and jumped inside. He put it in reverse and backed away, deeper into Green Isle. All I could think about was Bonnie and Clyde.

"Listen," Daro said. "They going to beat me up, and lock me up. I need you to keep this money," and he shoved the money he just got at me.

Now listen, I'm wearing a mini skirt, some flats, and a tight shirt. I was looking cute, but I couldn't hide any money. But I already had it. Daro was hiding the weed with one hand and driving with the other. I knew I couldn't put it in my purse. That's the first place they'd look.

So I stuffed it in my panties.

Finally, the police stopped us. They opened Daro's door and threw him out. A cop came to my side.

"Ma'am, get out of the car."

As I'm getting out, I can hear fighting from the other side. As they're handcuffing me, they throw Daro to the ground in front of the van.

"Baby, you see them beating me up?"

"Yeah, I see them,"

"Call my mama. Call my daddy," Daro yelled. He was face down on the ground, with his hands cuffed behind his back. I was so scared.

"You don't know who you're dealing with," one of the police said. "This is the Render family. They stay in trouble."

I'm sweating bullets. I know that Daro is going to jail. I'm handcuffed, my knees pinched together. All I can think is what if this $4,000 fall out of my thong?

I played the victim. I was going to college. I was working at Foot Locker. Daro told them not to lock me up, too. Unlike him, I had never been in jail. And I had four thousand dollars of his money.

"Prove it," one of the cops said.

I told them to look in my purse for my GPC ID card. When they found it, they saw that I was telling the truth. The officer looked at the little plastic card and then he looked at me.

"You are a nice, young woman and here you are messin around with this knucklehead," he said. "You know what? Do your parents know you're out with him? We're going to call them right now."

I didn't give them my mom's number though. I gave them my sister's. I thanked God that she didn't pick up. The only thing I said into the voicemail was "Call Bina."

Eventually, they ended up letting me go.

About that time, Daro's parents came pulling into Green Isle. His daddy raised hell.

"You better let my son go!" he yelled, but the police told him he better go on home.

They took Daro away, and I drove his van to his mama house. After he had been processed, Daro called from jail and talked to his dad. I didn't know it then, but he told his father how much money he had given me. When he asked, I gave him every dollar.

"You're a nice, young woman," Daro's father told me. "Trust worthy."

That night is when I had to give myself a reality check. "Bina," I thought, "are you going to go forward dating this guy, who has no intentions on leaving the game? This could happen everyday." I knew I liked him a lot, but I realized I loved that boy after I decided to continue dating him after that happened.

Things were good after that, for a few months. Daro stopped taking me on all of his plays and started thinking about who he let me be around. I was already living in the Brittany Apartments on Covington Highway, and he moved in with me. He were like best friends, soul mates. I started loving him even more, because I noticed he was making better decisions for my sake. He never stopped hustling, but he did start hustling smarter.

Even though we stopped doing everything together, one thing that continued was the skating. Since being with Daro, we had started going to Cascade Skating Rink on Sunday nights. Daro's cutlass had been finished for a while. It was navy blue, like midnight, with a white top. It had a custom, chrome steering wheel, that looked like rims. He had the engine redone, too, and big speakers in the back. Whenever Daro took me out skating, he drove that car, and on Sunday nights he brought his homeboy Dee Dee. Along with the people who would meet us there, that was our crew for skate night.

One particular Sunday started off like the others. I had my black skates with the black wheels, and Daro had his blacks with stripes. His car bumped all the way there, and when we got to Cascade, everyone turned their heads to see who had arrived. I was really enjoying the life of dating a hustler.

Inside, I split time on the rink skating with Daro to slow songs and time skating by myself, watching him with his crew. They skated in a line with Daro in front. His move was to shake his dreads. As the evening was going on, I was starting to notice a lot of whispering, a lot of women staring. Most of it came when me and Daro would sit down together after one of the slow songs. Among them all, I noticed two in particular. One was petite and light-skinned. She had blonde and black micro braids and a big mouth. The other was tall, thick and had a single gold tooth. She also seemed to be older than all of us.

Nothing happened that night besides all the whispering, but within a week the light-skinned one was working at my job. I found out then her name was Oshi Jones. Not long after that I found out Daro used to date her. Not only that, but she had been transferred from the store on Memorial Drive. It seemed weird that she had been transferred a week after she saw me skating with Daro at Cascade. It also seemed like she had gotten herself transferred on purpose to make my life a living hell. I had been working at Foot Locker since I was 15. I had enjoyed all the years up until that point. Until that day. Everything about my job there changed after she started working there.

The drama started right around the time that I figured out that Oshi was friends with the other girl from the rink that night, the old one with the gold tooth. She started coming up to my job with her friends, pretending like she was a customer. I found out her name was E. And I say pretending because she never bought anything. She was there just to intimidate and harass me.

One day, after two months of that, E came into the store with a bunch of girls who weren't with her regularly. It was worse that day that it had ever been. I ran to the restroom crying, and called Daro.

"I can't take it no more," I told him. "Everything is drama with you. Are you fucking these girls?" part of me wanted to know. "You already got a bitch that done got transferred to my job that I got to see everyday working my 8 hour shift. Making my life a living hell. And now your other bitch bringing her whole crew in here like, 'Bitch, I dare you to say something to me.'"

"Man," Daro said, "Hell naw. I'm finna come up there."

Daro was there in twenty minutes, flying into the Foot Locker. Him and Oshi started arguing. He started calling her all kinds of bitches, and that she better stop fucking with me. If not, he was going to send somebody to 'see aboucha.'

Oshi calmed down after that. And while I still saw E every other day, she only strut by the store entrance. She never came inside, but she made sure I saw that she and her crew were out there. Instead of staying depressed and sad, I decided to get even. One day after leaving a store meeting, I saw that Oshi had parked her mama beat up maroon van near my Escort. Back then I always kept a knife in my car for hood rats. I used it to stab two of her tires. I got the ones on the right side so no one saw me.

"Ha ha, you bitch," I thought.

Not long after that, on another one of those days I'll never forget, Daro came home and woke me up.

"Baby," he said. "Baby, look." When I looked, I saw a tattoo of my name on his leg. I started smiling. I almost wanted to cry, because I knew that was something a street guy would never do. He even had it in a place where people could see. When he wore shorts, you could see my name big as day. Any insecurities I had went away. I knew then that he loved and fucked with me.

Two weeks later, I had his name on my lower waist. Infamous Tattoos, across from the Candler road McDonald's. That day I felt like we were bonded, and would be together forever.

But here these hoes come again.

Fast forward a couple months, to another Sunday night. It was the same drill as always. You already know where we headed. Daro's cutlass is beating as loud as it can beat, and the car is just shining like chrome. He just had the white boy in Suwanee redo the engine, so the car is soundin real good, it had nice a roar. He was fresh. I was fresh. We were all fresh that night. When we get inside, the DJ is jamming. But after awhile I noticed Oshi, E, and Hope was in the cut by the speakers. I felt like something was gonna go down, and just had a bad vibe.

Now, Hope was D'Ron's baby mama and they had been together forever I had heard. D'Ron owned a barbershop inside a little service station plaza on Columbia drive, where Daro got his hair lined up once a week. In this little plaza, you could get a gallon of gas, an ounce, a pound, or even some white. And later, I found out how convenient all his hoes were. E stayed right next to the barbershop, and Oshi stayed on Panthersville.

So, as me and Daro were skating, they were all watching us. Oshi, Hope, E, and her crew. Like always, sometimes I'd be with Daro, for the slow songs, and sometimes I'd be by myself while he was skating in a line with his crew.

At one point, while I was skating alone, I got bumped from behind. I turned around to see it was Hope.

I said, "Bitch what's up?" I was ready for whatever was about to go down.

Hope said, "Bitch you know what's up. You keyed my car,"

"I don't even know what yo car looks like,"

"Oh you wanna play dumb. I got somethin fo yo ass,"

"Bitch you better keep rollin past me if you know what's good for you," I said finally, but Hope wasn't alone. I was. I skated directly to Daro and told him what happened.

"Man," he said, "Fuck them hoes," like it wasn't a big deal.

Five minutes later I was skating again, around the outer edge. I see E on the side line (the old bitch never skated, just showed up, started shit, then went home). I was determined not to move from my path. She was determined not to let me pass. As I went by, she grabbed me by the neck and started choking me.

I fell to the floor, and tried to get up, but couldn't, because I was on skates. Like a damn fool. E started punching me, and Hope, too. Somebody must've told Daro that I was in trouble, because after awhile he came flying in and got the hoes up off me.

He told me, "Go to your locker and get your shoes," so I did. I took off my skates and put on my shoes, and went to the bathroom. I saw that I was bleeding in the mirror. I had a gash under my nose and there was blood smeared on the side.

"Oh hell naw," I said to myself, then louder. I wasn't the only girl in the bathroom. Everyone had seen what happened. All of the spectators behind me filled my rage. "It's going down," I told everyone in the sound of my voice. All those girls left with me, like cheerleaders, like they was really bout to do somethin. From what Daro had said, I thought we were leaving. I thought I'd find him out front. When I looked around, I didn't see nobody but Hope, E, and her crew.

They talk shit. I talk shit. The next thing I know I'm on the ground. They punchin me. They kickin me. And the cheerleaders. Well, they weren't even cheering. They didn't do a damn thing. I was laying there thinking, "but you were my support system in the bathroom!"

After I don't know how long, here come Daro. Here come my superman. He bust E in the face, hit her so hard she fell on the ground. He got Hope off me, too, so I could get up. As I did, the police pulled up. D'Ron pulled up, too. Errbody had called errbody.

D'Ron was in Daro's face, "You up here beating on my baby mama? I don't give a fuck what they got going on, don't nobody touch my baby mama."

"I don't give a fuck," Daro shouted back, but it didn't go any farther than that. The police was there, like I said, and they had even brought the paddy wagon. They took us all to jail.

Before the evening had started, I had a fresh weave. When I got to the station, it was hanging half off my head. That's how they took my picture, with my weave hanging from my braids. The guard told me I had to take it all the way out before they put me in my cell. And I did as best I could, even though I never got to my cell.

Daro had the cash money bound us out, and we were gone in four hours. I assume D'Ron did the same for Hope. But E had to stay. We all found out later that they had a warrant out for her arrest.

The next morning I cursed Daro the fuck out. I told him I wanted to know the truth. To this day, I still don't know everything that was happening all around me back then. After that, I went to GiGi's hair salon. Half of the stylists and clients already knew what had happened. The streets were already talking and everyone knew how I got my ass jumped and beat. I patiently waited in the front until it was my turn. I purposely tried to be anti-social.

"Cut all this shit off," I said.

"No," Sabrina said, "your hair is still long, and I can treat the middle, Bina."

"Cut this shit off."

After she cut it, and curled it, she spun my chair around for me to look at my new haircut in the mirror.

"Oh my god," I said. "I'm still beautiful."

When I got back home Daro was still there, looking pitiful. We had a long talk, about how things had to change or I was leaving. After that, we never went back to the rink: there was too much of his past there, too much drama.

Things calmed down after that, and two months later, I missed my cycle. We bought two pregnancy tests and downstairs at his mama house we found out that I was pregnant. Even though it wasn't planned, we were both so happy and excited. That next week I had a doctor's appointment, and everything looked fine. We went back to his mama house and told the rest of the family.

A month later we went to the next doctor's appointment, and received devastating news. The baby wasn't forming right, and they had to force a miscarriage. Daro kept telling me everything alright but deep down I knew it was a disappointment for him, too. I just couldn't stop crying. Even though it wasn't planned, I knew he was looking forward to starting a family.

The morning that they forced the miscarriage, I was throwing up. It felt like I had been crying from when they told me all the way until we pulled up to Atlanta Medical. When they told me how the procedure worked, I was so disgusted and hurt. I never knew about the process of them destroying a baby, and I won't repeat it.

Losing Daro

Things slowly went back to normal after we had to force my miscarriage. Things weren't always good, but they weren't always bad, either. I was right back at work, and sometimes my hours weren't very consistent. Daro's schedule was strange sometimes, too. He had to go when he had to go if it meant making money. Mostly, I didn't think anything of it.

One particular day I had worked ten or eleven hours. I was tired, worn down. I just wanted to lay in the bed. Daro had told me he was going to shoot pool with his friends, which was something he didn't do too often at night. I remember him going out at about 1-1:30 then coming back around 2:45. I didn't say anything. All I thought was that it was a little quick. In my sleep though, my conscience was working.

When I woke up that next morning, I just felt like something wasn't right. It made me want to start snooping. Daro was still sleep, and I was careful not to wake him. I took the dog out, and when I got back I decided to be inspector gadget. I noticed Daro's clothes downstairs, and when I looked closer I saw a brown stain on his shirt. It was the kind of stain that made you want to look closer and smell it. It was sweet smelling, but I couldn't say exactly what it was. I did know that something wasn't right.

I crept upstairs, and saw that Daro was still sleep. I grabbed his phone off his nightstand then went back downstairs. I already knew I was going to see something I didn't want to see, but I just had to know what was going on. I took his keys, went outside, got in his car, and pulled off. I didn't want him waking up and taking the phone, or leaving.

Daro never locked his phone, which had made me trust him more. Later, I realized that was him crossing his T's and dotting his I's. He had slipped up this time. Sure enough, he had been out with some woman at a hotel. I wasn't sure how everything went down, but it must not have been as pleasant as he wanted it to be. As I went through the texts, I noticed that he was texting a woman named Cole, and I guess they were supposed to meet up. It was the hotel next to Malcom Cunningham on Snapfinger. He had evidently met her there. All of the texts were short. I don't know exactly what happened, but I know he met her there, and then came back at 2:45.

I sped back to Lakeshore. He had already called me ten times, and was waiting for me at the door. I immediately confronted him. As I got out of the car, I was cursing. I threw his phone at him, and his keys. He went right into another one of his lies.

"Man, I ended up getting a room for Lil Jr. He asked me to get a room for him."

"What the fuck was that on your shirt, it sure smelled like chocolate syrup?"

"Man, that was hot chocolate from Dunkin Donuts,"

"Okay since you got the room, let's go to the room."

I don't know if he talked to Lil Jr. while I was getting ready, but when we got to the hotel, Lil Jr. was there at the room. Daro said I was trippin, dropped me off back at Lakeshore, and went to his mama house. He didn't say anything else to me about the chocolate stain, or the woman in his phone.

So we were having trust issues. I found it difficult to trust him, but I wasn't the only one that was insecure. While all this was going on, I was still in school. I spent time there in study groups, sometimes late into the night. And sometimes guys would be in those groups. Sometimes those same guys would get my number, and call me. Daro didn't like that. I think he thought I might have wanted a more educated man, because I was around them all the time. A man that wasn't just street smart, but also book smart. A man working on something that could lead to a career, a 401k, all the things a business man might have. Not just a hustler that had no plan to stop hustling, or plan at all. It seemed like all the insecurities we had with each other could have created room for someone else to come in.

One particular night, I had cooked him his favorite dinner. The evening was going nice, then the phone rang. It was one of the guys from the study group, who did like me. A lot. The conversation started off about the project we had done, but the semester had been over for weeks. He started asking me personal questions. Daro was sitting right there listening. I tried to be as discreet as possible, tried to get off the phone as quickly as possible. Daro snatched the phone from me.

"Who da fuck is this?"

The guy just hung up. Instead of having my back, instead of saying anything. Then he texted me: Call Me. Now you know that made it ten times worse.

We immediately started fighting. Screaming and cursing at the top of our lungs. We're physically going at it.

Daro is yelling, "You know what, maybe it's best you be with that nigga from your school. You do you, like how I'm doing me."

I'm crying, "I don't want to be with him. I'm not doing me. He only had my number because it was a class project. He made it a personal call. I can't help who likes me."

Daro wasn't hearing any of it. He stormed off, saying he wasn't coming back. He told me not to call him. I was crying as I ran after him. He didn't give a fuck. He almost ran over my foot driving away.

I ran back into the house, desperate and distressed. I didn't know what to do. Everything was innocent, and I was about to lose the person that I loved. I called him. He turned his phone off. All around me, our apartment was wrecked. It was like things had broken and couldn't be fixed.

I went upstairs and got his gun out of his nightstand. I guess at first I was doing it only for his attention. Like hey, I have this gun, will you please listen to me? Can we work things out? Everything was innocent.

I called Daro again, and this time he answered. I was crying so much, I could barely talk. All I wanted was for him to listen. "Come back home and talk," I said.

"I'm never coming back," he said.

"I have your gun. I don't want to do anything crazy,"

The next thing I heard was dial tone.

That's when I made an impulsive decision. I didn't care about nobody but him. I was preparing myself to end my life. I stopped crying and found a blank sheet of paper. I wrote a note, saying I loved him, but he wouldn't listen to me. I told my mom and my family that I was sorry, and that I knew they wouldn't understand, but I felt like I didn't have anyone at that moment. The note was done, and I had Daro's gun in my hand.

But I was too scared to do it.

So I took the letter, and the gun, and got in my car. I was determined to talk to him. I was driving so fast. I could've been hit by a tractor trailer. I could've hit a person. This was the worst point in my life. Nothing in my life mattered, not even me. I had to get to him to let him know I didn't do anything. How could we ruin three years of our lives over nothing.

When I got to his mama house, I left the note, but brought the gun. I tucked it in my jeans and walked to the door. I rang it, but no one answered. I walked around the side to the downstairs bedroom window. I could see that there were people in there, but not clearly who they were. I moved to the next window. I could see Dee Dee, Daro, and Daro's brother that hardly ever came around.

I took the gun out of my jeans and beat on the glass with it. They got scared, not knowing if it was the police or whoever else.

Everything happened so fast. This was the moment that changed my life.

Daro ran outside. Dee Dee ran outside, but went back in when he saw it was me.

"That phone call sounded real suspect," Daro said. "I don't trust you. I want you out of my life."

I starting crying again, saying, "You give me a lot of reasons not to trust you," but he looked like he had already made up his mind that he was out. I think if I was guilty, I wouldn't have been that desperate. But because I hadn't cheated, because everything was innocent, I was so upset. I felt like he was my everything. I couldn't go on without him.

When he turned around, and I saw he was willing to leave me in the middle of his mama yard, I told him I didn't want to live.

He never turned around.

I took the gun and pointed it at my stomach. Well, I thought I had pointed it at my stomach. I just remember a loud bang and a shock to my body, and immediately falling to the ground. I saw Daro turn around, and instantly fall to his knees. He was yelling for Dee Dee to call 911.

The blood was coming out so fast. The bullet felt so hot, but it was like I was freezing at the same time. Daro picked the gun up, then threw it back down. He was scared and didn't know what the police would think, so he picked it back up to rub the finger prints off the gun. It was his gun, but I had the bullet. The gun was probably hot. I know it wasn't registered. I laid there in a puddle of blood, fighting for my life. Daro kept walking back and forth panicking. I'm sure he had a thousand different thoughts in his head, and wasn't sure what the police would think.

Right about then is when his parents pulled into the driveway. His mama came running over to me.

"Oh my god, what's happened to Bina?" Dee Dee had already called 911 by this point. Daro mama called them again.

I didn't know it at the time, but one of my lungs had collapsed. It was hard to speak, and I started losing my breath and tears rolled down my face.

"Don't call my mom," is what I said, then, "don't touch me," when Daro tried to pick me up.

The ambulance came, along with the police. The paramedics took me, and the police took Daro.

"Man, I didn't shoot her," he told them as they arrested him, "she'll tell you I didn't shoot her." He went to the precinct, and I went to Grady.

To this day, whenever I see an ambulance or a fire truck speeding off to somewhere, I always say a prayer that they make it in time. They are such a blessing to whoever they're helping. If not for those paramedics that night, I would've died.

"Can you speak?" They asked me. "What's your name?"

I could see them, but I couldn't see them. I was halfway gone, and fading. I was a perfect stranger to them, but they saw courage in me that I didn't see in myself. I felt myself dying, and I was willing to go. They did whatever they could to save my life.

When the paramedic asked my name, I told him, but he didn't hear Tashbina. He heard Tasha. And that's what he screamed all the way from Daro mama house all the way to Grady.

It made it easier to keep my eyes awake, and the next thing I knew they were wheeling me in. They hooked all these things to me. The bullet was five inches from my heart, and it had worked its way through my body. They were trying to take it from the back.

"Put me to sleep," I screamed. I was in so much pain, covered in blood. It felt like I was on fire. "Put me to sleep. I don't want to be awake." I don't know if they gave me a shot, or if I passed out from the pain.

When I woke up, there were several people next to my bed, looking down at me. All I could feel was shame. I had disappointed my family, my friends, because I hadn't thought enough of them to call when I was at my lowest point. When they saw that I was awake they started praying and crying.

The first thing my mom said to me was, "Tell me what happened. Did Daro do this to you?"

"No," I said. "I shot myself."

She didn't say anything else. She started crying. I started crying.

It's like bad news spreads faster than good news. It was like everybody had called everyone they knew and told them that I was in the hospital because Daro had shot me. I learned later that the arresting officer when to Towers with my sister and he looked her number up to let her know, and my sister is the one who called my mom.

So, my family was in the waiting room. Daro's family was in the waiting room, too. The police later found the letter I wrote in my car, but I never told anyone about it. There was so much speculation going on, but no one knew the whole story. Because I thought I had shot myself in the stomach, that's where I told them the pain was. They had cut me open to look for something that wasn't there, and it left a scar, but I had shot actually shot myself five inches from my heart and they took the bullet out of my back. My life could've in seconds over nonsense. I could blame no one but myself.

The shooting was the night of December 27th, 2005. I was discharged on the 4th of January, two days before my birthday.

My recovery went very fast. I went from barely being able to walk to walking in time to celebrate my birthday. Standing up straight was harder, but that eventually came, too.

We went to Carrabba's for my birthday. I was a little embarrassed, because I didn't know how my friends and family thought of me. I didn't know if they were sitting at the table thinking I was selfish, thinking that I loved Daro more than myself. I was glad to be there, and blessed, but I didn't enjoy myself.

Two weeks later, the staples came out and it was back to basics. My relationship with Daro was never the same. I could never tell what he was thinking. If he wanted to leave me. If he trusted me. If he thought I was psycho. Speaking of, I was glad I didn't have to go to the 9th floor at Grady. They evaluated me and decided what I had done was on impulse. They did recommend I see a counselor for two months. After my six week visit, she wished me the best, and said it was up to me to continue on.

No one could tell me what I didn't already know. I knew that I should never love a man more than God, or myself, and that I had too many people in my life not to pick up the phone.

Daro and I stayed together. I'm not sure what would've happened had I not shot myself, but because I did, it was like we were frozen. As time went on, Daro was still a little distant, and I was slowly getting back into the groove of things. I had finally gone back to work, and school. I felt like people were looking at me differently, like they could tell I had taken my innocence away.

Plus, our lease was almost up at our apartment. We started looking for new places, but after awhile it felt like finding a new place wasn't a big priority for him. I was feeling like he wasn't sure if he even wanted to stay with me. I could hear him thinking like, "Should I stay? I mean, she did shoot herself," but even if he wanted to go, he wasn't sure how. I was thinking that he might've been to scared to leave. I started looking for apartments on my off days, by myself.

Then Valentine's Day came. Now, I work in retail so on holidays like that I always work a 9-5 shift. I couldn't wait to get off to celebrate with Daro. When I left work at 5, and I was walking out to the parking lot, I saw a limo parked next to my car. The window rolled down, and I saw Daro.

"Hey, Baby, jump in," he said.

"What about my car?"

"Don't worry bout all dat," he told me. So I got in, cheesing and smiling. He could be so sweet. He had a bottle of champagne, and we toasted to a better year. I felt like, right then, things were finally getting back to normal between us. But you know the evening didn't stop there. He had already made reservations at one of our favorite spots to eat, Beni Hana's. After dinner, he showed me a silk blind fold and said, "I got another surprise for you."

When I took it off, we were in front of the Marriott. When we got to the hotel room, I could see rose petals, red and white, from the door all the way to the bed. On the bed, they were in the shape of a heart. He had all my favorite lotions and perfumes from Victoria's Secret, a birthday card, and a bunch of chocolates. The Jacuzzi was already running, too? Well, we all know how that night ended.

A month later was the day I'll never forget. It was a busy day for me, as usual. Class in the morning, work in the evening. Daro had dropped me off, and I hadn't been at work for more than an hour or so when Daro had called me on my lunch hour. He sounded excited. He said someone had called him about buying his car. I knew Daro was excited because if he sold his car, he'd be able to buy the black Cadillac escalade that he always wanted. I was so happy, because his birthday was in four days. I knew he was working hard, and I wanted him to get what he wanted.

"Baby, if I sell this car," he told me, "I'm gonna get you those coach boots you wanted." That's how Daro was.

I called him back at about 2:15 because I was so excited about him selling his car. It just kept ringing. I hung up, waited five minutes, then called again. I ended up repeating this three more times, and I was starting to get pissed because I knew Daro. Even if he was busy, he would still pick up the phone.

"Hey, Babe, I'm in the middle of something, lemme call you right back," he would say. With me calling like I was, it was irritating. I called his mama house.

"Hey, have you talked to Daro. He said he was going to meet somebody to sell his car," I said.

His daddy is the one who picked up the phone. He told me, "Yeah, he came to the house to get the title, then ran out." I hung up with his daddy and called Daro two more times. At that point, I was more worried than pissed.

Five minutes later the phone to the store rang. I'm assuming that it's Daro finally. It wasn't. It was Cassla, his sister. Crying and screaming. I could barely understand her.

"Bina, somebody got Daro,"

"What do you mean somebody got Daro,"

"Somebody called and said they got my brother,"

"What? I don't understand. What are you talking about. I don't understand,"

She hung up. Holding the phone, standing there, all I could do was try to process her words. Thinking back, I guess maybe it was more like I didn't want to understand.

The phone rang again as soon as I hung it up. That was the call that changed my life. It was Cassla again. I don't know what happened, but I could understand her that time. Someone had shot and killed Daro. Right then, as we were speaking, he was lying in his own blood at Wellington Court on Flat Shoals Road. I immediately started crying and screaming.

There was nothing that I could do. It's different when the person is shot, but on their way to the hospital. When they're dead, there's nothing to do but cry and wonder why. Daro had dropped me off. I couldn't get to Flat Shoals, not as quickly as I needed to. I called any and everybody seeing who could come get me. I called my mom, crying, trying to tell her what happened.

"Bina, I told you. Dating a guy like that, this is what happens," she said. It wasn't the time to be having that conversation with me. I hung the hell up on her and called Sheedah. I told her what happened, and that I needed her, ASAP. She came and got me, and we sped to the hospital, both of us crying.

His family was already there in the waiting room, some of his homeboys too. People were crying, punching walls. I learned that they couldn't let the family see the body until they had cleaned him up. I knew I didn't want to see him with a bunch of blood on him. He had died from three gun shot wounds, one to the stomach, two to the face. The doctors said had he been ten pounds heavier, he would've lived.

I sat there waiting with everyone else, thinking about how a few months earlier everyone had been in the same room waiting to see me. We ended up leaving two hours later, then left and went back to Daro mama house. On the way there, I got a call from a number I didn't know. It was Hope, apologizing, for my loss and everything she had put me through. I was polite, but I also wasn't paying it much attention right then.

There were so many cars at the house. I sat down at the family table, where we always sat, and just listening to the house full of people cry. I remember at one point the hospital called, asking if they could have Daro's eyes. His mama cursed them out, yelled and cursed and screamed at them. I just remember thinking how selfish that call was, because everything was just so fresh.

A week before, I had gotten one of those giant birthday cards for his birthday. Cassla had asked me to get it, and I had also reserved a cake. It had pictures of us, and pictures from his childhood. We were going to surprise him at Joe's Crab Shack. Cassla decided we would continue on, and have a cook out in his memory.

I knew that everyone would be there, and I had prepared myself to see his exes, even the women who wanted him but could never have him. I just wanted to keep good spirits, because even though he wasn't there, it was still his day.

The card was sitting on the family table, and I was one of the first people to sign it. I thought carefully about what to write, because I didn't want to offend anyone, and I knew that everyone would see what was written there. I wanted to keep it short and sweet, because he already knew that I loved him.

"Daro, you will never be forgotten. You are our angel. We'll always miss you. Love, Bina."

So, the day went on, as people came in and out of the house, paying their respects. I had gotten something to eat. As usual, his mama had cooked everything. It was delicious, too. There, in that house, doing something casual and normal, I felt like I had found some good space where I wasn't in tears. I didn't feel good, but at least I wasn't crying.

That's when I made the mistake of reading what others had written.

My eyes were drawn to the message left by some woman named Cole, "Daro, you were my soul mate. I don't know how I'm going to live without you. You were my soulmate."

Who the fuck was this? After that, I started reading all the comments. No one else had written something like that. Not even me. I was pissed off, my face was red. I was determined to find out who this woman was. I knew she was in the house.

I immediately went to Daro mama and pulled her to the side, saying I needed to talk to her. We ended up in one of the bedrooms.

"Who the hell is Cole and where is she?" is what I said. I knew I was upset, because of how I was talking to his mom in her house. Thinking back though, I don't feel so bad, because all she told me was lies. She told me Cole was showing the brothers and sisters houses, and I did find out later she was a real estate broker. She wasn't just a real estate broker, though. She was a real estate broker that was deeply in love with my man.

I left from there and went back into the main room, casing. I was remembering when Daro cousin had cracked the voicemail when we were trying to figure out who killed him. When moving through the messages, there had been a woman speaking, and then a little girl, and Daro cousin had quickly moved to the next message. Was that Cole? Was the whole family in on it?

I was looking around for anyone that had brought a little girl, and eventually I found her.

It was shocking when I met her, because I never thought Daro would sleep with or even date an older woman. Cole was blonde-headed, but she was mixed with something else, to this day I still don't know what. She had big breasts (probably implants) and an ass that was out of this world. She wore long nails with white tips. She looked a little conservative, but could still get ratchet.

It really made me think. Was this a real cougar? Was she the fine older woman who only dated younger men, took care of them and give them money? Was that money used to take care of us and our apartment? Was her outside appearance what had drawn him in the first place?

In the midst of all my questions, we all left to go to South Dekalb Mall to get t-shirts made. I saw Cole jump in the car with Cassla. I thought about Daro mama, and then his cousin, and now his sister. The whole family had known about Cole, I realized, and they had been keeping me in the dark. I was pissed off, looking like the fool. I was angry to think that they had kept the fact that Daro had a chick on the side away from me. The thought that maybe I wasn't even the main chick started creeping up in my mind. But who had he lived with for those years? Woke up next to and laid down with? After everyone had their shirts made, I went to my mom's house. Everyone else, Cole and Cassla and the rest of them, went out to Red Lobster. I decided then to begin to distance myself from the family.

Cole spoke at the wake, brought her little girl with her to the podium, where she talked about how much Daro loved her mama. Cole spoke at the funeral, too, rode in one of the black escalades the family had rented for the occasion. I was his girlfriend, and I didn't even know they had planned that. I thought it was sweet, because of how much Daro had wanted his own escalade, but them not telling me hurt. It made me think that while I was distancing myself from them, they were doing the same thing to me.

The worst of it was when they even went so far as to suspect that I had something to do with Daro's death. But that's for another time.

The final piece of the puzzle came when I went over to Daro mama house, one of the last times I was there. I noticed Cole was there, too, paying her respects like I was. I left when she left, and decided to follow her to where she lived. Wouldn't you know it, she stayed two streets over from D-Ron's barbershop, that convenient little spot where he could get his hair edged, but also see Oshi, or see

E. See Cole, then be back to our apartment before I even suspected. I had to just shake my head and keep driving, move forward with my life, and focus on the things that I could control.

Starting Over

Sometimes life will seem like a 360, and people who used to wish evil things on you can end up being friends when you need them. And sometimes haters, liars, and cheaters are just haters, liars and cheaters.

Not too long after the funeral, I got a phone call from Oshi. Even though she had caused so much chaos between Daro and me she seemed to be a little support system for me after he died.

"Bina, I know you're grieving," she told me, "and I know things are still a mess, but how 'bout I pick you up tonight and we go have a drink?"

All I wanted to do was stay balled up in the house crying, but I recognized that I had to get out and do something if I was really going to get on with my life, so I gave in.

It took me about two hours to get ready because I spent a lot of my time second guessing myself. Should I go? Should I not go? Could I even trust Oshi? It was one thing to listen to her on the phone, but it was another to put myself in her hands. There was no way to know if she was being genuine. Sometimes people will get all up in your business to transfer your business to someone else.

But I had already agreed. The only thing left to do was go. I tried to put my worries out of mind as I looked at myself in the bedroom mirror. I had my signature look, Chinese bangs and long hair. I even went with red lipstick that night to make me feel even sexier. For whatever pain I had, it would pass.

Oshi picked me up and we went to the club. With my hair blowing in the wind, my spirits were lifting. Change what you can change and move on, I thought to myself.

South Beach Bistro off Roswell is where we pulled up too, when Oshi and I walked in it felt like all eyes were on us, like we owned the room. We walked to the bar, to get our drinks. We were both looking pretty fierce, so of course the drinks were free. As I was standing there, looking around, my song came on. I immediately hit the dance floor, music was always my escape from things. I was backing that thang up, completely in my own world. For a moment, it was almost like my worries were gone.

Now, something I've always believed in is letting a man be a man. When I looked up I saw three guys looking at me from the stage, I just gave a flirty smile, but then turned back around to dance with Oshi. If a man thought I was attractive, he should just come over and say hello.

After my song went off, we went back to the bar for our second round. When I turned around, I noticed that the same group of guys were still staring. One of the guys kept smiling and waved for me to come to the stage, he introduced himself as D Town. I didn't know who he was, but I found out shortly. He was a local Atlanta producer, originally from New Jersey. What I liked about him was that he didn't come at me with a bunch of game. He just let me know that he thought I was pretty, asked if I was dating anyone, and if we could exchange numbers and get a bite to eat the next day. Men have to realize that women don't want game. It doesn't take all that to get a number, just keep it short and sweet. After we exchanged numbers, and I finished my drink, and me and Oshi continued enjoying the night.

The next day we had that bite to eat, and I finally started taking steps to get on with my life. There were still days when I cried, but it seemed like there were just a few less tears each time.

I didn't tell D Town because I wasn't ready then, but looking back I really think he was the friend that I needed at that time in my life. Someone who didn't know me to judge me, and who could provide a shoulder to lean on. There were still a lot of things going on involving Daro's family, and I tried to keep D Town away from the chaos, but it found us anyway.

The first incident came when we were leaving his house one day. He didn't live anywhere near where Daro lived, or was killed, but there was a flyer on his car asking for any information he had about the murder. There was a $10,000 reward and a phone number listed. D Town was about to throw it away when I stopped him. I felt like it was time for me to tell him what it was all about. We sat in the car while I told him the story. I let him know that my boyfriend of three years had been killed, but not just killed. His family thought I had something to do with the murder to the point of hiring a private investigator. The part of the story I didn't know at the time was that Oshi had gone back to the family to tell them about D Town, and everyone believed that I had knew him before Daro's death. Even though I had just met him, Oshi knew the truth but what was said to Daro's family was a lie.

But you know they say, people come into your life for reasons, seasons, or a lifetime. D Town took everything I said and just listened quietly, and when I was done he acted like I hadn't said anything strange. He just asked me where I wanted to go eat. I was really surprised how much he was there for me.

The second incident occurred late one night, after a long day at work. After the three flights of stairs, I stopped to see black spray paint all over my apartment door. In huge letters it read, 'you gonna die, bitch,' along with

Daro's name several times. I didn't know what to do, but I knew I didn't want to go into my apartment. I burst into tears. The first person I called was D Town, and I told him that I was on my way to his house. I felt terrible driving over there, because I didn't want to always be bringing him bad news, people following us etc. When I got to his house, he told me he wasn't going anywhere, and was going to be beside me 100%.

There were even other things going on that I didn't find out about until after the fact. I had distanced myself from the family after I found out about the private investigator, realizing that Cole meant more than I did. I had to find out about Daro's father's incarceration on the news. Mr. Render couldn't deal with the loss of his favorite son and had turned into a madman over trying to find clues about the unsolved murder. On September 4th 2008, he was sentenced for murder. When I watched the news and saw his mug shot and heard about what happened, I fell apart, and was just sad for his father and family. I know Daro was looking down from heaven just shaking his head, his father had committed murder and his favorite uncle had passed all within a year of his murder.

After the spray paint incident, even more things happened and had me very paranoid. On this particular Sunday evening I had just left the jewelry store and had arrived home around 6:45pm. My normal drill was coming home to take a shower, change my clothes and head out. I hated being alone because it made me face reality, that Daro was really dead and that I didn't feel at peace. I quickly got dressed and headed out.

When I was leaving out the door, I heard a sound from the stair case. I looked down the small space to see if I could see anything but I didn't. As I proceeded to walk down to the second level, there was a guy standing in front of a door. My heart immediately started pounding fast like it was about to pop out. I knew something was about to happen! I looked at him and said, "What are you doing?" he said, "What are you talking about? I'm waiting on them to come to the door." I was not convinced and my conscience was never wrong, but I was too scared to walk past him so I proceeded back upstairs. As soon as I started going upstairs, he ran after me. I started running and trying to get my keys ready to open my apartment door; he was on my tail and I felt as though my life was about to change forever. I managed to get in my apartment but when I went to slam the door, that's when he pushed his way in. I screamed and we fought and he grabbed my butt and arms, I continued to scream and cry. He let me go and ran to the door and left out of my apartment. I couldn't catch my breath and I immediately called the police and told them to meet me at a gas station near my apartment. I ran to the window then to the stair case to see if he was there, then I took flight down to my car and sped off.

I drove to the BP gas station on Covington Hwy, and called the police again. They told me to stay there and they would meet me at the apartments. Of course, there were no signs of him so they wrote up a police report and said they would continue the search. I called D town to let him know what had just happened and he told me to come to his house. Even though I was still shaken about the whole situation, all I could do was keep thanking God for allowing him not to rape me. I was confused as to why he didn't: was he scared that someone would come because I was screaming and yelling so loud? Or was he on drugs and always admired me and just wanted to put his hands on me?

As I pulled up to D town's apartments, he was outside waiting on me. He had went to Walmart to buy me a bat. I laughed through the tears thinking of how cute that was but preferred to have a gun. I stayed at his house for several days then had to go back home for more clothes. I went back to my apartment around 11:30am before I had to go to work at 12:30pm. I looked around, got out my car, and ran up to my apartment as quickly as I could. I grabbed a bunch of clothes and proceeded out. When I got to the bottom level, I seen the same asshole again standing ten feet from my car. This time he had his pants down jacking off. Instead of me being scared, I pushed his ass out the way and got in my car. I called the rent office and told them to look out the window and they told me they were calling the police and I said to them great and I'm also breaking my lease. They told me I could move to another apartment. I laughed because I stayed right by the leasing office. Wasn't that the safest place?

After that happened, I moved in with my sister. I had been on my own since I was 15, and I was very used to being on my own, but this was a time when I needed my family the most. So there I was with my sister, her husband, and my new baby nephew. Things quickly became a mess. My sister gave me rules, like she was my mother. I had to be in by midnight, and had specific chores to do on certain days. I know my sister wanted to protect me, but it really felt like I was in jail. It was actually D Town that got us to sit down and work things out. My sister agreed to let me stay over at his place a couple times a week, so she let up some. Even though I started staying the night at his place, I still took things slow. I wasn't ready for the physical stuff, and he made me feel like I was worth the wait.

The night we finally decided to take it to the next level, as I was getting aroused, I called out Daro's name. This of course immediately stopped the intimacy. He was upset that I had called out another man's name. I was upset because I realized I still wasn't over Daro. I put on my clothes and left, but he stopped me before I pulled out of his apartments. We sat in my car and talked for hours. It was things like that, looking back, that really made me think D Town was exactly what I needed in my life during that time. I needed someone to help me put the pieces of my life back together.

D Town had a friend named R Love, and me being green I didn't know how successful and popular they were. They hung out together, casually and professionally, and the more time I spent with D Town the more I felt like I could trust him, but little did I know. My friends always called me Inspector Gadget, and my exes would tell you the same. Sometimes people won't tell you everything, so you have to snoop to really find out the truth.

One particular day, D town and I decided to spend the entire day together, running errands, little things like that. We had gone to the Bank of America on Panola Road. D Town ran inside to take care of some bank business, and as I was waiting in the car, I saw some bank statements in the cubby hole by the door. I picked them up to read them, and I'm glad I did. I noticed he had spent $400 at a place called the Body Tap, which I immediately Googled. The next statement had a similar amount spent at the Foxy Lady. Everybody knew about the Foxy Lady on Moreland. I started to feel like I was at the same point in my life again dealing with sneakiness. Again I had so many questions and this time, though, I was going to get answers.

When he came out of the bank and got back into the car, he saw the mean mug on my face.

"What?" he asked.

"This is what," I said, and dropped the bank statements in his lap. Like every other man, he went into automatic defense mode.

"Man, why you going through my shit?"

"Don't worry about all that. Why are you going to all these strip clubs to see these dancers? You never told me once you were going to the strip club. I had to find out from your bank statements. It's obvious that you love going to these places, spending hundreds and hundreds of dollars every week."

He saw how upset I was, and I think he might've known how ready I was to end things. It wasn't going to happen like last time. I was determined. He put on a sympathetic face, saying, "Baby we just go to have fun after working hard in the studio. Those women don't mean anything."

His saying that made me feel better right then, but I knew it was some bullshit. I was starting to get the same feelings I got when I was with Daro. I knew I had to make better decisions for Bina, and get out the relationship early when I saw similar signs, before it was too late. I had to be absolutely certain though, so I decided to continue my snooping. I didn't want to leave a good man for one bad thing, but if I found anything else it was time to burn rubber.

Later in the same week, my opportunity came. He had fallen asleep, and left his phone out. I needed to find out if he was really going to the strip clubs for fun, or if he had a favorite dancer. Everything starts with a thought, then lust takes it from there.

First I made sure he wasn't just cat napping, then I jumped off my side of the bed got on the floor and crawled around the bed over to his side. I grabbed the phone and went into the bathroom in the next room, and locked the door. Just in case he woke up, and saw his phone gone, and wanted to snatch it from me he couldn't.

They say if you go looking, you'll always find something. D Town had many women in his contacts, but I didn't get mad immediately because they could be artist or even business partners. The name in the phone was Julce, and the conversations they had back and forth were about whether or not he was coming, how much he missed her and that he was coming to the club. I made up my mind then to go to Body Tap and find out who this woman was, I wanted to see how she looked.

That next Wednesday I was there. I went on Wednesday because that was Body Tap's main night, so I knew she'd be in the building. I went to the bar and asked for a drink, and also asked the bartender, "Do you know if Julce is here tonight? I want her to dance for me."

"We don't have no Julce here," the bartender said.

I hadn't put two and two together that Julce wasn't her real name. I was starting to get pissed off and irritated that I couldn't find her. I asked somebody else, and they said the same thing. I was getting tired of looking so I gave up on searching that night.

I also told D Town that the relationship wasn't working. I couldn't trust him, and was starting to believe that he wasn't at the studio all the times he claimed to be, that he was wrapping up sessions early to have other engagements. It made it even more difficult because we weren't having sex, he claimed he wanted to live right way, so after having sex twice, we stopped cold turkey and this was very difficult. So when I found out about all this madness, it didn't make since to me and made my decision easier to move on with my life.

So, that was it for us. I don't have any regrets, though. D Town was really what I needed in my life at that time. He gave me time when I needed it, someone to listen to me, and had my back when the going got tough. I believe God bought him into my life for a season, that season helped me move forward and cope with Daro's death..

The Devil's Plan

It was nice for my sister to let me stay with her and the family, I mean, she didn't have too. Even though we didn't have the best relationship, she did really always try to have my back. It was a really nice gesture. On the other hand, I had been on my own since I was 15, so used to being able to do what I wanted to do, when I wanted to do it. The problem was, sometimes what we want to do, isn't what we really need to do.

So I left my sister's house. I wanted to be on my own, and that's exactly what I got. Very quickly I fell into desperate need. I was still working at the bank, but it just wasn't enough. I had pawned all my jewelry, asked multiple people for loans. My tab was getting long, though. I looked up one day and realized the first of the month had already come. I had to think fast.

Now, I've always had faith that god would take care of me and wouldn't put anything on me that I couldn't handle. But how do you know that when something is put in front of you, that god put it there? When I was thinking fast, one thought that came to mind was Diamond from the movie the *Player's Club*. Sometimes you gotta do what you gotta do to get yourself out of certain situations, I thought to myself. I really felt like I was at that point. After I had made my decision, I tried not to think any more about it. I just called up some girls that I already knew danced.

"Oh no, not you Bina," they all said.

I just asked them if they had any extra clothes that would fit me, shoes that I could wear. I had put my feelings, and my faith, behind me.

So there I was, in the Strokers parking lot, on Brockett Road. It's the place where lots of dancers start. I remember shaking and sweating. I had to talk to myself just to get out of the car.

I had never been inside of Strokers, and always wondered what it looked like . Ever since I was young, I can remember that big pink stiletto that was on their building. Now was my time to see what it was all about. I changed my walk like I was already a dancer. You know, that stank walk.

When I walked in, I seen the stage first and pool tables to the left. All the customers and all the girls turned to look at me. Deep down, I wanted to turn and run back outside.

"Bina, you got to pay this rent. You gotta pay what you owe to all these people. I focused on my obligations as opposed to my shame.

I asked for the daytime manager, a man named B
Dave. I went to the bar and waited for him to come out.
All of a sudden, I saw this big white guy, and when I say big
I mean big. Not fat big, muscle big. He told me to follow
him, and when we got to his office he said, "You know the
drill."

"Excuse me?" I said.

"Pull up your shirt and pull down your pants."

"This is my first time…"

"I gotta see your body, honey."

I felt like a dog at the vet, getting an exam. He told me
I had a pretty hot body, and I asked him if he had any open
positions for a waitress. That's what I preferred. I told him
I was in a situation, and needed some quick money.

"Well, you're not going to make the kind of money
you're talking about just being a waitress." Then he told
me I needed 300 dollars for a permit, and I could start that
night. He must have seen something in my face. I didn't
have the money, that's exactly why I was there. I just looked
down, about to leave. "What's wrong, you don't have it?"

I just shook my head. I felt terrible.

But then he told me that he'd give me a money order
for the permit.

"Are you serious?" I said, then I paused, "I don't have to
do you any favors, do I?"

You seem really sweet, and desperate. I just
ut."

...ke I was saying, we all know this wasn't God's
...n for me, but I still started feeling better about my situation. I ran out of there and drove to the courthouse on Memorial Drive, got my permit, and started getting ready for that night.

My friend Rhonda told me I needed to get my makeup done, and she also gave me a checklist for the things I would need. Bring your own towel and washcloth, she told me, and pack lashes, shaving cream, a razor, and baby oil gel. She had also given me four outfits that halfway fit. My ass cheeks was out most of the bottoms and I didn't have breasts so the tops were big on me. But I had to make it work.

That night I walked in for the night shift and got stopped by the lady in front.

"20 dollars, please," she said.

"Oh," I said, "this is my first night."

"Oh, okay, you cute. Head to the back."

As I went to the back, guys were already pulling on me. With my clothes on. I knew it was going to be a long night, but I hoped it was going to be a good one. I needed to pay my bills.

So when I walked into the dressing room, I see there's like 80 girls . I was so nervous, it seemed like everyone knew I was the new girl. I found a place for myself, and

took my clothes off. I was immediately glad I had brough
my own stuff, because I didn't want to have to share.

That's when I learned that every strip club has a house
mom. What's a house mom? She's a lady that is called mom,
and sells everything a dancer would need to get ready, like
wash cloths or eye lashes. Body oils, body washes, and flat
irons were free, but you still have to share. Strokers even
had a candy lady who sold hot fries, taffy, chips, everything
you probably shouldn't eat before you go dance.

I remember the house mom asking me what my dance
name was. I said China Doll, but she replied that it was
already taken, along with Black China. I had to think
quickly because she was trying to put my name on the list.
What I didn't know then was that we had to sign in under
our name, and the time determined what fees we had to
pay. Everyone always complimented me on how pretty and
exotic my eyes were, so I decided to call myself Asia.

After that I did a quick wash up while these girls was
staring at my booty. A couple of them slapped it on their
way out. I started feeling like I needed to show these girls I
wasn't a punk, so after the second slap I said, "Bitch, don't
touch me." The other girls looked up and started laughing.
I wasn't sure what was so funny, but I didn't get slapped
again. The stares kept on though. I could feel everyone
wondering who I was dating, what got me in there, and
how desperate I was to get what I needed.

time to go out and make some money.
little outfit. I walked out onto the floor,
too nervous to ask any customers if they wanted
dance. I also noticed when I got on the floor that the DJ was calling the girls' dance names to go on stage. I hesitated again because I did not want to go on stage. I had the face, I had the body but lords know I didn't have the moves, the moves that these professionals had.

I went to the DJ booth but stopped when I saw other dancers in there with him. I wanted to talk to him alone so I waited patiently, and watched them sit on his lap and play around. I felt like the longest wait ever, even though it was a couple of songs. When I finally went in, I begged DJ Slim not to call my name because I did not want to go on stage. It was my first night and I was still learning. I didn't want to get embarrassed.

He told me, "Man, Shawty, you gotta go up there. You'll get a fine if you don't go."

"Really?" I asked, "Why would they make me go up there?" I was there to make money, not lose it. I walked off distraught, and tried to figure out what I was going to do when I got up on stage. I started watching the other girls' moves. It was obvious what I was doing but I had already tried to get out of it. I would just have to learn. I watched girls hit splits, or climb the pole. One of the best dancers there was White Chocolate. She always put on her patent leather thigh-high boots and rinsed the pole off with rubbing alcohol before giving the show of the night. She would make $1,000 by herself was considered VIP, which meant no one danced with her while she performed.

It felt like my time came around way too early.

"Asia! Hollywood! Cola!"

I ran to the dressing room, trying to hide so he would skip over my name, but he didn't. He continued to call for me.

"Asia! Asia! Asia!"

It looked like I had no choice. I quickly put another outfit on and said "Fuck it." I walked out onto the floor with a harder twist. I walked onto the stage, grabbed the pole, and struck a pose. On the outside I looked confident, but on the inside I knew that whatever I did, I could not leave the pole. It seemed like I was on stage for four hours but really it was only four songs. The only thing that made me feel a little better is that I had two other girls on stage with me, so all the attention wasn't just on me. I still think the customers knew that I was the new girl, though.

We only made $20 a piece for our stage set. I had sweated through my outfit, and gotten my hair soggy. I had to do another wash up, wash my hair, blow dry, flat iron, touch up my make up, and put on my third outfit.

When I got back out onto the floor, I just stood at the bar and smiled, waiting for someone to come get me.

Eventually, a few dancers came over to the bar. We struck up conversation, and I told them it was my first night, but I think they knew. It felt like everyone had seen my stage set.

"Girl, you not gone make no money like that if you think these men gone come up and ask you. Closed mouth don't get fed," one of them told me.

Looking around, I realized she was right. I noticed all the girls with stacks of money were walking around asking. All the girls with no money were over at the bar with me. That's when I decided I was going to do what I had to do. I felt like my being on stage was the more embarrassed I could feel.

I'll never forget this one guy. He was older, with glasses, and kind of nerdy.

"Hi, how are you?" I asked him. "Would you like a dance?"

He looked at me and smiled, "you must be new."

I laughed, "How did you know?"

"Because no one ever says hi, how are you?"

I immediately felt embarrassed.

"But sure, go ahead."

I remember taking off my top, then taking off my bottoms. I looked up at God and whispered for Him to forgive me. I knew I wasn't the best dancer. I wiggled my legs, then bent over and grabbed my ankles, shook my butt. I looked up at him and saw that he was smiling, and guessed I was doing okay. He danced me for two songs, which totaled ten dollars, because Monday nights are five dollar nights at Strokers. I looked at the ten dollars and got my answer about how long the night was going to be. It was only 8pm and the shift didn't end until 4am.

By the end I had blisters and my body was so tired. I had made $210. I could barely stay awake, but my obligations were my motivation.

"Keep it going," I kept saying to myself.

Fast forward a week, and I was starting to get used to things. I had brought three more outfits that actually fit me. I was looking pretty sexy, and on this particular night I owned the room. I had asked everyone from the DJ to the bar tender to dance, even the guys over in the corner shooting pool.

You know those pool sharks that play in the club every night. Well, the big time one was Rick, light skin, bald head. From what I heard, he had all the money and all the girls. At first, I was dancing for his friend, and while I was doing that another guy was looking at me and when I was done he called me over. I went over to him and he complimented me on my smile, said I looked so innocent. He asked me what I was doing there. I replied that sometimes life will put you in situations where you gotta do things you don't necessarily want to do. He asked me to explain.

"I'm not going to tell you my whole life story in the strip club," I told him.

"Well tell me outside the strip club, then."

I had made a vow to myself. I was not going to give these men my number, wasn't going to date, nothing. I had one purpose: to get what I needed and get out.

He danced me the entire rest of the night, and as the evening turned into morning I told him more and more of my story, and more and more of my situation. My vow broke before daybreak. He told me to call him. He said he could help me.

Five days passed. I was tempted, but told myself no. I didn't want to get caught up. I danced for three more days, went to work for three more days, went to class for three more days. That week wasn't as good as the previous one. The phone number was shimmering like gold.

When I called, a deep voice picked up.

"Robbie speaking,"

"Hey, Robbie. This is Asia, from Strokers, did I catch you at a bad time?"

"No, Love, it's the perfect time, how are you doing?"

"I'm good, just came from the gym,"

"Well are you up for getting a bite to eat?"

"Sure, where did you have in mind?"

We met at Pappadeaux off Jimmy Carter. As I was driving there, I had a million thoughts in my head. What was he up to? Was he being genuine? What was he going to ask me to do? What was I even doing meeting with him? I was scared and nervous.

I walked in and he was already sitting at the bar.

"What's up, Robbie," I said, and sat next to him.

"You, baby," he said. I could tell he was used to trickin' because he had that trick talk. He got right down to business and asked me how much I needed to get me out of my situation.

I hesitated because he was just that straight forward, but I told him the number.

He didn't pause at all, just said, "When we doing this?"

"Doing what?" I said. It was like I knew, but didn't want to know.

He started laughing. He described it as "a favor for a favor."

We met up the following day. I made sure to get his money first, so I told him to meet me at the bank. I deposited the money, and we proceeded to my apartment on Memorial Drive. I had never had sex with anyone except people I was in relationships with. I wanted to back out, but knew I couldn't. It was like I was losing another piece of myself. I felt like a prostitute. I was remembering the part in *Set it Off* when Jada Pinkett had sex with the man to help her little brother.

After he got up, he said two things. "It was good," right at first, and then, "I'll call you later," after he had washed up in the bathroom, and after he had put his suit back on. Then he was gone.

After the door closed, I started crying. Another part of me was gone, but I finally had what I needed to leave the club and never look back. I cried tears of sorrow, but also relief.

But… I didn't leave the club. Sometimes God gives you exactly what you need, but the devil convinces you that you want more.

Asia and Korea

I've always been real hippy, but never had any breasts. I looked like a boy when I laid down. Breast implants were something I always wanted, but never could afford. With all the dancing I was doing by night, and the work I did for the jewelry store by day, I was able to save up enough money to pay for them. Everyone always told me that I didn't need them, but this was a decision I made for me, and no one else.

I remember the day of my consultation, waiting for them to call my name.

"Tashbina, we're ready for you."

I followed the lady to the back, where she told me to take off my clothes. She handed me a robe and told me the doctor would be right in. I was excited, but I was also anxious about what to tell my mom and my sister. They were both very judgmental, and it wasn't easy to open up to them about certain things.

First off, they thought I was only waitressing at the club. I went over to the house the Sunday after the consultation, and my mom made one of my favorite meals. We sat down to eat, and we were a few minutes into the meal when the question came out.

"Bina I just wanted to ask you because I don't want you to say I never asked. Are you stripping?"

I remember turning really red, and saying, "No, why would you ask me that?" I felt terrible, lying to my mom, but I knew she wouldn't understand. At the same time I didn't know why I was still at the club myself, the strip club is just like the street life it's a trap.

Things got quiet after that. I hurried up and ate my food then went to the bathroom. I cried for ten minutes. Through the tears, I saw myself in the mirror, and I felt like the worst person ever. I was in the bathroom for so long she came to ask if I was okay. I didn't want her to see my face, so as soon as I got out the bathroom I told her I needed to work on a project for class. I felt like at that moment she knew the real answer to her question, and was waiting on me to tell it. A mother always knows.

The next morning I decided to write my mom and sister a long email, about the breast implants, and how it was something I had always wanted to do, and that they didn't have any say in the matter. I had already paid half the deposit and was moving forward. I didn't want them judging me, but I also wanted their support. I was shocked, because they told me if that was what I wanted to do, then they were behind me 100%.

My surgery was at seven in the morning, and my step dad took me of all people. When Lee and I pulled up to the Swan Center in Alpharetta, I started getting nervous.

"Don't me scared now, B," Lee told me, then, "Or, we could always go back home."

I told him no, that I had paid $5700, so I was having the surgery. We both went inside and sat down to wait for the lady to call me back for the anesthesia.

Finally, they called my name and took me to the back. All I really remember is being in the gown and laying down. They said I'd be out in a few minutes. Before I fell under, all I could think about was what if something went wrong, what if I didn't wake up. Even though I had googled that only 2% of cosmetic surgeries ended in death. So I just calmed myself down and went to sleep.

I woke up screaming. My chest was tight, and burning, and I was in so much pain. I screamed so much one of the nurses came back to check on me.

"Honey, are you okay?"

"No!"

She asked me if I wanted my step dad, but I told her he wasn't going to keep me from screaming. In the next bed over was this Asian lady who had also just woken up. She wasn't crying out at all. The nurse didn't know what to do, so she got me in a chair and wheeled me out. They had three other patients in the lobby waiting for their procedures, so they just kept wheeling me out until I was out of the building. I guess they didn't want me scaring the other patients. Thinking back on it now, I'm laughing. I was the only one hollering from having surgery.

We went to McDonald's, because the nurses said I would need to eat. I got a kid's meal. Cheeseburger, no onion. I took my medicine with the food, and cried the whole way home. I stayed over my parents' house because I had no one to take care of me.

My mom and sister were waiting when we got back. I was still crying, but I smiled when I saw them. Lee helped me out of the car, and the two of them came over to see, but there was nothing to look at because I was covered in bandages.

My mom saw my tears and said, "What you cryin for? This what you wanted ain't it?" She always knew how to say the wrong thing at the right time.

So after a week at my mom's house, it was time to get back to the jewelry store. I had a hump in my back but I was ready to go back to work. It was still a month too early to go back to dancing though. I just wasn't ready for it, but one of my home girls from the club, Miracle, called me and told me it was time to get out of the house. Miracle was the type of girl every man wanted as a side chick. She was bad big titties, a very, very small waist, fat ass, and a face to die for. She had a certain way about herself, was very flirtatious. She worked at clubs where she didn't have a lot of competition, Pin Ups, Blaze, and Strokers. I liked hanging out with her even though she was the complete opposite of me, but we had a common ground the strip club. She told me she was picking me up and taking me out. I threw on some jeans and a cute, silky top. I was still wearing the surgery bra that the doctor had recommended I wear. My breasts weren't looking too hot, and I had on flats.

When I got into Miracle's car, she took one look at me and said, "Girl, where are you going?

"What?" I asked.

"Oh I have to get you some clothes to change into."

She took me to Atlantic Station, where her and her friends had a secret condo that none of their dudes knew about. Miracle showed me the closet and I saw pumps in all different sizes. She gave me a leopard blazer to put on and shoes to match. After that we proceeded to hit the streets.

I didn't know she was taking me all around the world that evening, but she was driving so I had to hang. The first club was Central Station. OMG. That ghetto place where hoochie mama, drug-dealing, super star wanna be's hang out. We stayed in that place for ten minutes, cause I complained the whole ten minutes. After that we went to Pin Ups. Now, Pin Ups was also ghetto fabulous, but it was also a strip club plus I knew some of the dancers there.

It was so packed that night the only place for us to stand was by the pool tables. Everybody knew Miracle, cute face, slim waist, and you know what else. So she had left me standing there while she went and talked to all her friends and customers. I saw two guys near me sitting at a high table. I could tell they were the lame 9 to 5 guys because they weren't getting any dances or getting up to tip the stage, and I thought I'd just call them out on it.

"Why y'all not getting any dances?"

"Because we didn't come to get dances," one of them said.

"So why did you even come?" I told them they could at least get up and tip the stage. This was the dancer's workplace. They laughed at me, but I was determined to state my opinion. Whatever I kept saying must have worked, too, because one of them got up and threw $20 on the stage.

A little after that, Miracle showed back up.

"How long you gone be talking to these lames?" she asked.

"I don't know. Why?"

"One of my homeboys want to meet you,"

"Who?"

Miracle pointed out this brown-skinned guy, a little heavy set but still built nice, maybe 5-11. He had a nice face, too.

I told her I'd be over there in a minute, then I turned back to the guys I had been talking to. I told them the reason I was saying all those things was because I was a dancer, just not at that club.

Then I walked over to Miracle's home boy.

"Hey, what's up?" he said.

"Hey, how are you?"

"I was waiting for you to stop talking to those lames, because I was about to head out."

We talked for another ten or fifteen minutes before he had to go. After he walked out of Pin Ups, I went and found Miracle, and she told me we were headed to Dirty Rats next.

"Oh hell naw," I said. "I'm going to church in the morning."

"No, I'm not taking you home," Miracle said.

All I knew is that I didn't want to be out all night. If Miracle wouldn't take me, the only option I had was for her home boy to take my home. He was nice to talk to and didn't seem like a psycho. I asked Miracle if she trusted him, and she said he was cool and I would be fine, then I told her that I was going to get him to take me home if she wouldn't. After that, I left out the club and saw him leaving in a black corvette. I flagged him down.

When he finally stopped, I told him, "I know you don't know me, but I gotta go to church in the morning. Can you take me home, please?"

The ride home wasn't too bad. We got a chance to talk more, and that's when he told me he had a girlfriend. I got quiet for a minute then, and I basically told him that I would never knowingly date a guy who had a girlfriend. Then he hit me with the line that every man says to make a female feel like its okay to keep talking to him even though he's in a relationship, "but I'm not happy."

"Are you a street guy?"

"What are you talking about?"

"Oh you know what I'm talking about."

Instead of answering then, he laughed, and told me he would tell me later. Right then we pulled into the apartments where I stayed. We exchanged numbers and I thanked him for driving me home, and he told me he would call me tomorrow. If only I had known then what I know now. I had told myself that I would never date another street guy, and his dodging my question should've been enough.

But life is full of tests, and some of them can take us by surprise if we're not paying attention. That's what it means to be vigilant.

As time went on, and I got my health back, I got deeper into the life. I was noticing all the extra attention my new twins were getting me. Before them, I always got a lot of attention, but now I was attracting even more. It confirmed that it was time for me to leave Strokers and start working at the real money clubs, places like Magic City, Cheetah, Onyx, Pink Pony, and Body Tap.

I remember the day I drove into the parking lot with the yellow, black, and purple building. I was a little nervous, sitting in my car. I knew I'd be competing with beautiful women used to making thousands a night. I went in to see the manager, whose name was Rich. He told me the same thing Big Dave had told me, so I pulled up my shirt and pulled down my pants. I had been in Big Dave's office feeling so embarrassed, but now I was almost happy to show off my new breasts. I wasn't worried at all about that part of the interview, but Onyx was the kind of place that made the girls audition.

Rich made me dance to three different speeds of song, slow, mid tempo, and fast. Everyone knows that I'm not the best dancer (ha ha), but my face and body were exotic enough to make customers want to look and spend money. After Rich said yes, I sped downtown to get my new permit. I was going to be dancing the following night. Later that evening, I met with Jaz to make me new, custom outfits, because I knew what I'd be up against. If Onyx was what they said it was, I was expecting to make $3,000 that first week.

That first night, as I entered the dressing room, the pink walls stood out. Girls were all over the place, and there were tons of lockers. I already knew the house mom, Brina, from the shop I had been going to for years, Set it Off on Candler road. It turned out, I wasn't as nervous as I thought I was going to be. When I took my clothes off, everyone still stared though. Not only because I was new, but because no matter how beautiful you are, people will still look for your flaws. I had the surgery scar on my stomach, and my new breasts hadn't fallen into place yet. I couldn't wait to put on one of my new outfits. I was going to give them something to really look at.

That night I didn't own the room but I still stood out. I left with $700 after tipping DJ Nando and the house mom, which was pretty damn good. It seemed like Onyx was how I had heard. What I had to learn the hard way was all the extra rules. You had to pay the DJ at least 20, and that was only if you had a horrible night. If the floor men walking around saw that you were having a good night, you'd better tip 50. If not, you'd have a $100 fine the next day you worked. As far as the house mom, you had to give her 10 even if you didn't buy anything from her.

Something else I learned was that Onyx girls formed cliques. There were the lame girls who walked around the club and danced more for the professional men, and did a lot of the VIP services. There were the ones in the middle, like myself, who would make good money dancing all night, but had their limitations. Then you had the celebrity girls. These were the ones that were picked by the singers, rappers, football, and basketball players when they came in. And after they had danced for the celebrities, they were the girls that were invited to the after parties at mansions, and upscale hotels. They would dance there, too, and sometimes have sex. They were making club money and private party money.

And even though I told myself I wouldn't get involved with the cliques, I did start hanging out with particular women, inside and outside the club. My crew consisted of Miracle, Juicy, Honey, and Stallion. I hung around each of them for different reasons, but all loved to eat, have martinis during the day, and loved the money were making.

While all this was happening, the guy I had met, Miracle's home boy, and I were getting closer. People called him B and he was from East Atlanta. We started hanging out more frequently, always going to Esso's, the Velvet Room, and Dream back before it was the Mansion. I learned quickly that dancing and having a relationship was a no-no. B knew all the guys with money. His home boys consisted of West Side Kris, Yank the Bank, and Flank. B knowing everybody really limited the people I could dance for, and restricted how much money I could make on our main nights. Not to mention that I had vowed to God to never date a street guy again because of what happened with Daro, who I still thought about on a regular basis. Life is so small here in Atlanta. As it turned out, D-Ron was B's personal barber, and he would come to B's house to cut his hair and line him up. One day I showed up at the spot and seen D-Ron. I froze like a deer in headlights. I didn't say anything, and I knew that D Ron would later tell B all about what had happened with me and Daro. B never said anything, just waited for me to tell him on my own. There were so many signs that the relationship was cursed before it even started, but I had already started developing feelings for him. Sometimes when you think you're moving forward, you're really moving backwards.

On one of my off days, he had picked me up and we were having lunch at Strip at Atlantic Station. I was enjoying the breeze outside, along with my favorite cocktail, Amaretto Sour. After lunch, we went downtown to Walter's, because B had to get the new Jordans. After that he told me he needed to run by his mom's house. I freaked out, because I was not dressed appropriately to meet this man's mom. I wasn't hoochie, but my shorts were short, and I just didn't look mom friendly. If I had it my way, I would've had on a knee length skirt and a nice silk top. I knew how to look classy and elegant, I just wasn't looking it on that day but B insisted.

I already knew what his mom would think when I stepped out of the car. There we were, in the driveway, and we were going back and forth about me going inside to meet her. He insisted that we go inside and dragged me out of the car and pulled me to the front door. As he rang the door bell, I started sweating. She opened the door a moment later. She was a short little brown skinned lady who loved to wear her hair in a bun or braids.

"Hey, how you doin?" I started to think then that B was forcing her to meet me just like he was forcing me to meet her. She continued to stay nice and cordial, and our first meet and greet turned out nicely.

Weeks later, that Easter, B introduced me to his entire family, including his two daughters. This was my first relationship with a guy who had kids, so I knew it would be awkward for me and for them. I remember walking in and everybody looking me up and down. One little boy said I looked like one of the girls from the video and that I was soooo pretty. Still, it seemed like no one was ready to meet me, but just like with his mom, B forced the issue. It made me feel like the family wasn't over his ex, Hennessey, who is someone to this day I've never seen, but I know for a fact she's seen me. From what I heard of her, she was dark skinned, had a beautiful shape, and long, gorgeous hair. What I was told was that her face wasn't the cutest but her shape made up for it. She was the woman B was with when he met me, 'the relationship he wasn't happy in.' Chasing me was the reason B wasn't going home, wasn't answering her phone calls, or giving her the respect she deserved. They say what goes on around comes around. What I did to her was the same thing that was done to me.

Eventually, his family grew closer me. His sister She-she was one of my favorites, she always admired my make-up, weave, and exotic look. She was really sweet to talk to and I enjoyed giving her my secret tips on how to keep it together. I liked his mom, too, who was a lot like my mom, who would say whatever was on her mind. It wasn't always a good quality, though. One time, for instance, I was over her house one Sunday after dinner, and we were all sitting on the couch. B was saying something I didn't like, so I responded to it. His mom told me that I needed to learn when to be quiet. I responded to that, too, saying that I was always going to say how I felt, and that whoever I was with was either going to learn to respect that or leave. It was all crickets after that. The funny thing is I think I was growing on her, and she was definitely growing on me.

I came time to tell B about my past some months after that. My feelings had deepened even more, and I didn't want to feel like I was lying to him, plus I felt like maybe he was waiting on me because of what D Ron told him. No one knew the whole, honest truth about my past, and the way I felt about B then, made me not want to hide anything from him. I told him about Daro and how that relationship had changed my life. I told him that I had made my share of bad choices, even tried to kill myself. He took everything I told him and said it was okay, and that he wasn't going anywhere. That was the second time that had happened, and just like the time before I felt like B was exactly the lover and friend that I needed.

And just like the time before, problems weren't too far behind.

On the one hand, because of the fast life I was living, I was definitely in another tax bracket. With the job at the jewelry store, and the one at Onyx, and being with B, I was able to pay for classes each semester, and other things I wanted, not just the things I needed. On the other hand, I was leaving the club at four am, was taking classes from 7am to 11am, then working at the jewelry store from noon to nine, only to be back in the club dancing at 10. I don't know how I did it, and I started to question why I had to do it. I even started to resent B for not telling me to slow down, not to burn myself out. I was hoping he would say it every time we hung out, or that he loved me enough to tell me to stop dancing, that I didn't have to do it anymore.

But that's only where the problems started. We started to argue more, too, about his not communicating with me, and how I was dancing for people he knew. One particular day we had a really big argument, and he hung up in my face. It started because I wasn't feeling like he made me a top priority on my days off from the store and dancing. I noticed that he was being a little too friendly with the other dancers, and some of the dancers were too friendly with him. I put it all together after two days of not talking after he hung up on me. I went over to his place and we made up how we always did after fighting, then I went to the bathroom to get myself together and noticed a pair of eyelashes in the trash. B's friends all called me "Bina Matrina" because I had a mouthpiece and looked like Trina, and B for one knew I didn't play that shit. I snatched the lashes out the trash can and immediately started going off on him.

I asked him about the lashes and he immediately became defensive, just like D Town, just like Daro. He said he had been gone on the road that his home boy Jr had been staying at his place, and had his girl over. I told him to call Jr, and as usual Jr stuck up for B so it would look like I was crazy and he wasn't cheating on me. In the middle of that particular fight, I started to think that I needed to self-reflect. All the guys I had dated had similar traits, all were fine, all had money, and all were cheaters. I had to wonder why I kept attracting these kinds of men.

At that point I should've walked away. Instead, because of the lifestyle, because of my feelings, I got angry and didn't speak to him for weeks, and then he started saying things to make me feel better, and we were back together. Every time I would catch B in a lie, he would buy me something to make me feel better about the situation. I saw it, but I didn't realize, not then. The longer I stayed, and the more mess I put up with, the more comfortable he got, and the less he valued me.

By this time, I was also working at Kamal's 21, which was right down to street from Onyx. I only worked at Kamal's on their hot nights, which was on Wednesdays and some Saturdays. They already had a dancer named Asia, which was funny because Asia was Daro's little brother, Nick's, ex-girlfriend. So I couldn't use that name, so I came up with Korea. I actually started liking the name Korea more than my dance name, Asia, at Onyx, but I continued to use both. Even though I didn't work there very often, I still had my favorite crew I loved to work with, which was Truth, Pistol, Asia, Sinna, and Mimi, along with everybody's old time favorite Sugar, who had been around for years and years. Kamal's 21 wasn't as nice as Onyx, but was better than Stroker's. I liked working there because I liked the hood atmosphere, and the crowd was always live. Dancing there was pretty good money, even though Sugar would call whatever we made 'chump change.' She was used to the old school money, sometimes making ten or twenty thousand a night. Then there was Terry, who worked at the front door. All the men loved her. She always wore jet black hair, and had pretty eyes and had a gold tooth. She was fierce and some of the customers wanted her more than the dancers.

However all the money in the world couldn't buy me out of my problems. Things took another turn on one of those Wednesday nights.

"Korea, Truth, Sinna, and Pistol!" the DJ Stylz screamed. We prepared quickly to get on our stage set. It was Cool Runnin's night to promote, so every Wednesday was either the Bitch Slap Contest or a dancer's birthday set. Cool Runnin was hilarious and had a lisp when he spoke. It made him sound very challenged, but this man was very smart. I was the last one to get on stage because I had to close down the jewelry store this particular night, then had to speed to the club. This was a regular routine for three years, classes in the AM, work 12:30 to 9:30, and the club 10:30 to 4AM. I noticed that this girl was staring at me while I was on stage dancing. I got closer to see who she was, and I noticed it was Shay from Magic City. The funny thing that I thought of was that I remembered seeing her at Onyx the night before. Was this girl stalking me, or too nervous to tell me this bullshit, so here it goes:

"Hey, Baby, what's up?" I said, stepping over.

"Well, I got something to tell you. Basically, I think we're fuckin the same man."

"What? Who? It gotta be B because that's the only person I'm fuckin."

"Yeah," she said.

I said, "How long have y'all been sleeping together?"

She said, "For two months," and she said she was just at his condo on Monday night.

I felt so damn stupid, and naive of the whole situation. I jumped off the stage and ran downstairs. I was crying over another man who didn't respect me, and that also embarrassed me, and didn't have his side hoes in check. I straightened my face up so the other girls wouldn't see me crying. I threw my clothes on, so I could get to my car and curse B ass out!!! I was also pissed off because I wouldn't be able to split my stage money with the other dancers because I jumped off stage, then had to pay a $50 fine for leaving early.

"Yo bitch just came to the club to tell me we sleeping with the same man. What the fuck? Pick up the phone," is the message I left when I got his voicemail, then I immediately called back. Over and over again, but he didn't pick up that night, almost like he was afraid, or maybe he was busy gathering up his lies.

He called me the next morning though, after he had everything organized. She was lying. She was jealous. She was crazy. She was trying to get at him, not the other way around. At that point I think I was angrier at myself than him, letting the same thing happen to me over and over again. I took a two month break from him. It was long past time for me to get out of the life. I was doing an exceptional job at the jewelry store and things were looking good for me to transition to a higher paying position, but to do that I couldn't keep showing up to work sleepy. I had to make myself and my career the priority.

The Promotion

They say slow and steady wins the race. While everything was going on in the club and around it, plus being with B and that fast life, now was the time for me to really start making decisions that would help me grow and not hinder me. So I did what I do best, and stopped right in my tracks, and asked God, "Lord I need guidance, please help me get out of this turmoil." Meanwhile, I started weighing all my options, the good with the bad. Would I walk away from the lifestyle of fast money, fancy cars, my second family (the girls from the club), or would I walk the path of reliance, obedience, and become the woman I could actually be proud of, that beat the odds. I was starting to rethink everything, even college. I had been in school for years. I always wanted to become a lawyer, but was even restarting to rethink that. I had realized I was more in college for my mother than myself. I didn't want to disappoint her, but I was starting to lose drive, and was learning and planning on how to be successful in a lane I chose for myself. Looking back, I realize now that God was with me every step of the way. All I had to do was walk the path that was laid out for me.

I made some tough decisions, and one of them was to make that year my last year in the club. I would stay for one more birthday set, which was the one night of the year that was all about that one dancer whose birthday it was. For a set of songs, all the other dancers either had to help make money, or stay in the back, and every dollar that fell during that set belonged to the birthday girl and no one else. Everyone knew about the set, and the birthday girl didn't have to dance at all before her special event that evening or she could worked the floor until her birthday set to make extra money.

As I prepared for mine, I was really excited. I knew that this was going to be my last time to make this kind of money. I went and had a photo shoot to have custom made flyers, called the balloon place on Covington Highway, all the little details to make sure my event was a success. Despite all that, the set at Onyx didn't turn out too well, because the main manager Rich was out of town, and Cliff, the assistant, was in charge. He let some guy buy up ten thousand 1s before my set which was at 2 am, then the guy wouldn't let B buy any from him. I only made $2,000 that night. That meant my birthday set at Kamal's 21 was crucial.

The next day, which was Wednesday, at Kamal's 21 was my birthday set. B came and showed up and showed out. It turned out to be the best birthday set ever. He threw thousands and the crowd from the club definitely supported me that night. The next morning, I counted out all the 1s and I ended up making almost $12,000.

For those next few months, the last few months, I worked six days a week at the club because it was the end. I stayed on Red Bulls and 5 Hour Energy shots, and put fabric softener in my hair so my coworkers wouldn't smell the smoke from the club the night before. Despite how tired I was, I could look around and see that everything was happening at the right time.

My DM at the time was trying to block my blessings, but I had finally come to understand that no one can block what God truly had planned for me. I ended up being hired at the sister company. I had made my mind up to walk away from the club life to transition into the woman God wanted me to be, and He made things fall into place. B and I decided to part ways. He continued to stress me out, and I couldn't focus on what I needed to focus on because my relationship was a disaster. But even though we weren't together, he helped me leave the club. Even with his help, and the promotion, it was still difficult in the beginning. I had to seriously learn about budgeting, had to learn how to go to sleep before midnight. I had to stop looking like a dancer, and more like a professional businesswoman. I had to make better decisions about life.

But just because you're making better decisions, doesn't mean that you won't face your share of struggles. When I first arrived at the Lithonia store, there were two individuals that I didn't get along with. One man was very lazy and I didn't do well with lazy people. The other was a woman, and she was the top salesperson at the time, and she felt threatened by me. One thing I always say is people lie but numbers don't. At every company I've ever worked for, I've always been one of the top associates and with the jewelry store I'd always been in the president's club. I was determined to bring the same professionalism and dedication to this new store.

One particular day, a basketball player from overseas had come in and wanted to purchase an engagement ring. I gave him one of my best diamond presentations, then asked him some questions about the lucky lady and we picked out the perfect ring. I took his driver's license and we started the credit application. As I was in the middle of that, the pastor of my church, Kerwin B. Lee, walked into my store, out of all people. I had been attending Berean Christian Church for 12 years, participating in worship service, ushering every third Sunday, and involving myself in small women groups. When I saw my pastor I knew he was God sent. It was confirmation that despite all the trying times, I was in the place God had prepared for me. I called my manager over and asked her if we could switch. I made the turnover a smooth transition, then quickly walked over to where my pastor was, near the Rolexes.

I greeted him, saying "What up, cuz," which was a term we used often in our church, because we never met strangers. We're all cousins.

Pastor Lee replied "What up cuz," back to me, and, "So I see that you're a Berean."

"Of course," I said. "I've been attending for many years, back when it was the smaller church on Young Road." I asked him what had brought him in today, and he stated that him and Yolanda had just come off of a cruise, and that he had seen a two tone Rolex Perpetual Datejust, and it just so happened that we had the same one. He asked me if I could do anything on the pricing, and everybody knows at this particular store there are no sales or adjusting prices. He took down the price on one of my business cards, and he told me that the church anniversary was the following Sunday, and that the church had asked him what he wanted as a gift and had given him a budget. I came around the counter and gave him a hug, and he told me that he would make sure that I would get the business if this is what they decided to get him.

After he left I went to lunch, and when I got back I had a message. A Mr. House from Berean Church needed me to call him back as soon as possible. I was so excited and almost too nervous to call. I made sure to go to my manager before I called and asked her if anything could be done on the price, even though I knew what the answer would be. She told me to grab the Rolex and put it in the system, and it was $200 cheaper. My eyes lit up and got super big because I was going to be able to do something on the price after all.

I called Mr. House back and told him the great news, and he told me he would be over to the store in one hour. This was really big because I wasn't even supposed to be selling Rolexes. I hadn't even started my Rolex training, but my manager approved it.

She said, "This was supposed to happen to you. Not everyone's pastor walks into the store every day. Go ahead and make that sale."

So I had everything set up in our diamond room, the nice, dark-green Rolex box, the timepiece itself which I had already cleaned and steamed so there were no fingerprints. At this point I was just waiting on Mr. House to arrive, and really thanking God for answering my prayers and making this happen for me. It isn't every day a girl gets a $11,000 sale her second day at a new store. When Mr. House arrived, I showed him to the diamond room. I presented the Rolex to him and all the certifications and asked him would he like me to wrap it up. He said yes, and that he was so glad I was able to stay in their budget. I told him that I appreciated that they gave me the business and to make sure they had our company's bag when they presented it to pastor on Sunday, so all the members would know where to shop. Of course after Mr. House left, my co-workers were furious. Because I had sold a Rolex without being certified, and had closed two deals within a couple of hours. In addition to that, God seemed to have worked it out that the two people I couldn't stand, Mr. Lazy and Ms. Competitive, ended up leaving the store. Working hard and trusting in God to make a way continued to work for me.

As I did all these things, God started talking to me more frequently and more clearly. I was beginning to see when I stepped out on faith and became a better person, He really started making things happen for me. Selling was always natural for me, and it was easy for me to build rapport with my guests, and I guess my superiors thought so as well. Eight months into my working at the Lithonia store, I came into work one day and my managers Mrs. Green and Mr. Johnson let me know that the diamond department manager position was open, and let me know the responsibilities. Mr. Johnson in particular spent time guiding me to help me see that when I continued to do the right things, my blessings would overflow. I talked the promotion over with Mrs. Green and Mr. Miller, my district manager, and they both thought it was a good idea for me to become the new diamond department manager. What I really liked about Mr. Miller was that he sometimes saw the potential in me that others didn't. All it takes is one person seeing your potential to create an opportunity. I was so ecstatic that I couldn't do anything but call my mom and Lee so they could share in my promotion. My peers started to look up to me more after that. I think everyone could see me growing and making more responsible decisions. I felt good knowing that my hard work was really paying off. Dancing was quick money but when I looked in the mirror it was almost like I was looking at someone else. At Asia or Korea. Working at the jewelry store was slower, but I didn't have to hide and lie about what I was doing. I could smile in the sun. I was going to church more often, too, giving back to God by tithing and the more I went the more I realized it was something I needed. It helped me truly find myself.

I really saw myself blossoming, and I was learning that a piece of mind is priceless. A year after being transferred to the Lithonia location, I got another promotion and they sent me to Kennesaw. A higher volume store with a higher clientele. I was always an awesome sales person, but now was the time to be a better manager, and I'm still working on it to this day. The people I manage really test my managerial skills, but I've learned that without a test, there's no testimony.

My Wisdom to You

I wrote this book just for you, my sistas.

What I want you to take from this book is self worth and self efficacy. Life is about making the best decisions so you don't have to compromise yourself to live the life you want. So here it is, and this comes deep from my heart. I wish I was told some of this advice earlier…

To my young girls and young women out there… slow down! You have all your life to deal with drama and competition from the next, learn how to listen to those older than you! Some things you don't want to experience, trust me I know, you've read my story… Never love a man more than yourself or God, it will lead you to an empty place. Learn to take advice from people who truly love you and want the best for you! You don't know everything so go sit down and stay in your lane. Always remember books before boys 'cause boys bring babies, ambition before men 'cause they will always be there. Educate yourself and never be satisfied with the minimum because you will never reach your maximum, and a man respects a female more who can hold down herself and who has standards, so get some! Why settle when the world is yours! Live the life you will be proud of, unfortunately people never forget the story but you determine how it ends! Live each day like there's no tomorrow.

Sincerely,
The Angel Left Behind
Tashbina Wahid

Special Acknowledgements

To Mom and Lee, thank you for those living room talks, kitchen cries and those prayers that you said for me. There's nothing like a praying mother.

To Tierra D. Reid, my big sis, thank you for all the love and advice you gave me to make this happen. Even though I thought I knew it all, obviously I don't lol. To Keesh my sister from another mother, I believe you are my biggest fan.

To Laokham, Keyara and Quiana, my bffs, thank you all for being that listening ear, that phone call away, and helping me become a better friend. Couldn't forget my girl Rozina thanks for being you and being there.

To Pastor Kerwin B. Lee, thank you for the inspirational word you give every Sunday and Tuesday. It helps me get through those tough days and weeks. Also to Pastor Stewart, you came to the hospital to pray and lay hands on me when I almost left this world. I'm so thankful for you both.

To Ms. Hunt, Colonel King, Ms. Johnson and Ms. Clark, you kept pushing me and giving me the words of wisdom I needed to become the young lady that others look up to.

To G. Johnson and Ms. Cole not only were you great coworkers to me, G you gave me life changing advice. I know you thought I wasn't listening to you, but the whole time I was taking mental notes of how to become a better person and stop taking short cuts that would hurt me in the long run. Lillie I haven't known you long but what I do know is that you support me a 100% thanks girly.

To Mr. Billups, Ms. Brown, Mrs. Green and Mr. Miller, my bosses that made a difference in my life. Thank you for encouraging me to be the best at what I do and pushing me to keep moving forward. I will continue to make you proud, again thank you for seeing the opportunity in me that others did not see.

R.I.P. Daro Da Don
March 19th, 1982 to March 15th, 2006
In loving memory of Darold S. Render, the person who really
showed me what true love is, in spite of....
You cross my mind more than you know.

In ever-lasting love

Made in the USA
Charleston, SC
24 September 2013